Microcomputer Modelling by Finite Differences

Microcomputer Modelling by Finite Differences

Gorden Reece

Department of Engineering Mathematics
University of Bristol

A HALSTED PRESS BOOK

JOHN WILEY & SONS
New York

© Gorden Reece 1986

All rights reserved. No part of this publication may be reproduced or transmitted, in any form or by any means, without permission

First published 1986 by

MACMILLAN EDUCATION LTD
London and Basingstoke

Published in the U.S.A. by
Halsted Press, a division of
John Wiley & Sons, Inc., New York

Printed in Great Britain

ISBN 0–470–20739–6

For Nesta – who encouraged me to start this book and who would have loved to see it finished – for Miriam, Helen and David

Contents

Preface		ix
1	**Introduction: What this Book is about**	**1**
	1.1 Why numerical methods?	1
	1.2 The problems we shall solve	3
	1.3 The computer program	4
2	**The Finite-difference Method**	**7**
	2.1 Finite-difference methods	7
	2.2 Second-order problems	13
	2.3 The general second-order problem	18
	2.4 Graphics	21
3	**Convergence and Divergence**	**25**
	3.1 Convergence	25
	3.2 Divergence	27
	3.3 A cautionary tale	27
	3.4 Solving systems of linear equations	29
4	**Better Solution Methods**	**33**
	4.1 The general problem	33
	4.2 The algorithm — a smart trick	34
	4.3 The program revisited	36
	4.4 A neater algorithm	40
	4.5 Gradient boundary conditions	42
5	**Further Improvements**	**45**
	5.1 Non-constant coefficients	45
	5.2 Gradients at the boundaries	46
	5.3 The non-uniform grid	47
	5.4 The finite-difference equations	48
6	**More Ambitious Applications: The Heat Equation**	**51**
	6.1 Background	51
	6.2 A simple form of the equation	54
	6.3 The finite-difference form	54

7	**Two-dimensional Phenomena – a Glimpse of Reality**	**59**
	7.1 Heat conduction in two dimensions	59
	7.2 Deriving the heat equation	60
	7.3 The finite-difference form of the equation	62
	7.4 The model of k_{PN} etc.	62
	7.5 Boundary conditions	64
	Adiabatic boundary	64
	Fixed-temperature boundaries	64
	Finite heat transfer at the boundaries	65
	Gradient-type boundary conditions	66
8	**The THC (Transient Heat Conduction) Computer Program**	**68**
	8.1 Introduction	68
	8.2 The MAIN control segment (1–999)	69
	8.3 The START subroutine (1000–1999)	72
	8.4 The PHYS subroutine (2000–2999)	75
	8.5 The EDGE subroutine (3000–3999)	76
	8.6 The WORK subroutine (4000–4999)	78
	8.7 The PLOT subroutine (5000–5999) and the DRAW subroutine (9000–9999)	82
9	**Elementary Applications of the THC Program**	**84**
	9.1 Introduction	84
	9.2 One-dimensional problems	84
	9.2.1 Fixed temperatures at two ends of an insulated bar (RUN 9.1)	84
	9.2.2 Fully-developed laminar flow between parallel plates (Couette flow) (RUN 9.2)	85
	9.2.3 Flow in a circular pipe (Poiseuille flow) (RUN 9.3)	86
	9.2.4 The distribution of heat in an annular cylinder (RUNS 9.4 and 9.5)	87
	9.2.5 Cylindrical annulus with heat source (RUN 9.6)	88
	9.3 Two-dimensional problems	88
	9.3.1 The superposition principle (RUN 9.7)	88
	9.3.2 Fully-developed laminar flow in a rectangular-sectioned duct	89
	9.3.3 The electric potential inside an infinite box	90
10	**Further Applications of the THC Program**	**98**
	10.1 Update to allow for further modifications	98
	10.2 Applications with standard-type boundary conditions	100
	10.2.1 Rectangular intrusion	100
	10.2.2 Hollow square	100
	10.2.3 Non-uniform conductivity	101
	10.3 Non-standard boundary conditions	101

	10.3.1 Specified-gradient boundary conditions	101
	10.3.2 Sine wave along an edge	101
10.4	Modifications to the contour plot: standardised contours	102
10.5	Epilogue	102

Appendix: Full Listing of the THC Program for the IBM PC
(Apple II modifications listed in REM statements)   *115*

Index   *124*

Details of associated software diskette   *126*

Preface

Mathematics should be fun. Too many maths teachers spend their time convincing their pupils that maths is boring — and that it is difficult. I was lucky enough to be taught by people who enjoyed maths and who showed me how to enjoy it.

One of the most exciting things that has happened in my life-time has been the spread of knowledge and the removal of the mystique that used to surround the possession of some items of knowledge. I do not mean just particle physics or the structure of the earth's core — I mean things like how to mend a burst pipe, service a car, buy a house or deal with the taxman. A new generation of people has grown up that is not afraid to try things out for itself. Teachers and publishers have a duty to provide people with books showing them how things are done. 'Experts' have been reluctant to do this in the past — probably because they were afraid that their expertise would be seen to be pretty trivial once anyone could use it. The usual excuse was that people might misuse the information — well, that is our right.

Probably the greatest single liberator of the intellectual curiosity of ordinary people will be the microcomputer. It is possible to buy a perfectly good computer today for less than the cost of a new suit. With it there will usually come an excellent manual on BASIC. Such computers can be used for playing games, but far more excitingly they can be used to illustrate — even to solve — some problems in maths that would have been virtually impossible to undertake when I was born.

We have not even begun to explore the real capabilities of the smallest computers — in maths or in the physical and social sciences. Some attempts have been made to use computers in teaching, and a whole area of study (CAL: Computer Assisted Learning) exists, but CAL is probably only in its babyhood and has yet to reach its infancy.

This book takes subjects that have never been tackled in schools and are hardly covered in undergraduate courses. Using the simplest (or anyway the most popular) computer language, BASIC, and a knowledge of maths little beyond O-level, it illustrates most of the ideas with computer programs that can be run on most microcomputers. You will obviously have to make occasional slight modifications to handle the variations in BASIC dialects.

The spirit of this book is, I hope, entirely in keeping with the ideal of making the maths in it be fun. I enjoy it and hope you will too. The subjects covered are finite-difference methods and how they can be used to solve real problems in physics and engineering.

Among the many people who have contributed to this book by their encouragement or by reading and criticising what I had written are several of my colleagues and all the students who took my course in the years 1980–86. To them all, many thanks.

University of Bristol　　　　　　　　　　　　　　　　　　　　　　　Gordon Reece
1986

1 Introduction: What this Book is about

1.1 Why Numerical Methods?

In general, real-life problems do not have 'analytical' or 'exact' solutions. The whole idea of nice problems with nice solutions, using carefully contrived mathematical tricks is a historical freak. Mathematics has grown up the way it has, entirely because until very recently the simplest and most obvious methods for solving most problems were too slow to be of practical use. So two things happened: firstly, more complicated techniques were developed for special important classes of problem, and secondly the problems themselves were simplified, often to the point of triviality. The first course in dynamics (delivered inimitably by Professor – now Sir – Hermann Bondi) that I went to as an undergraduate began with the delightful suggestion that we should "Consider a smooth weightless elephant . . . ." Figure 1.1 shows such a 'classical' elephant, actually weighty rather than weightless, standing (unsuccessfully, of course, in the absence of friction) on its smooth inclined plane.

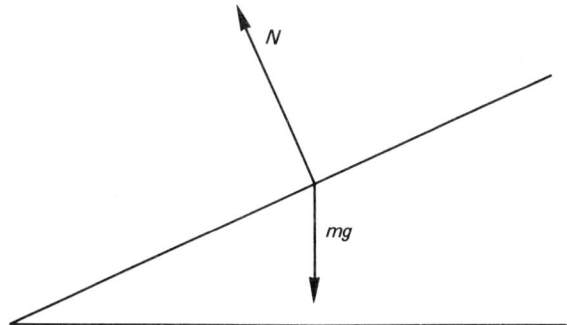

Figure 1.1 The classical elephant

Happily we need no longer assume our elephants to be smooth or weightless. This book deals with hairy, heavy, real elephants. Figure 1.2 shows a real elephant attempting to stand on the same inclined plane.

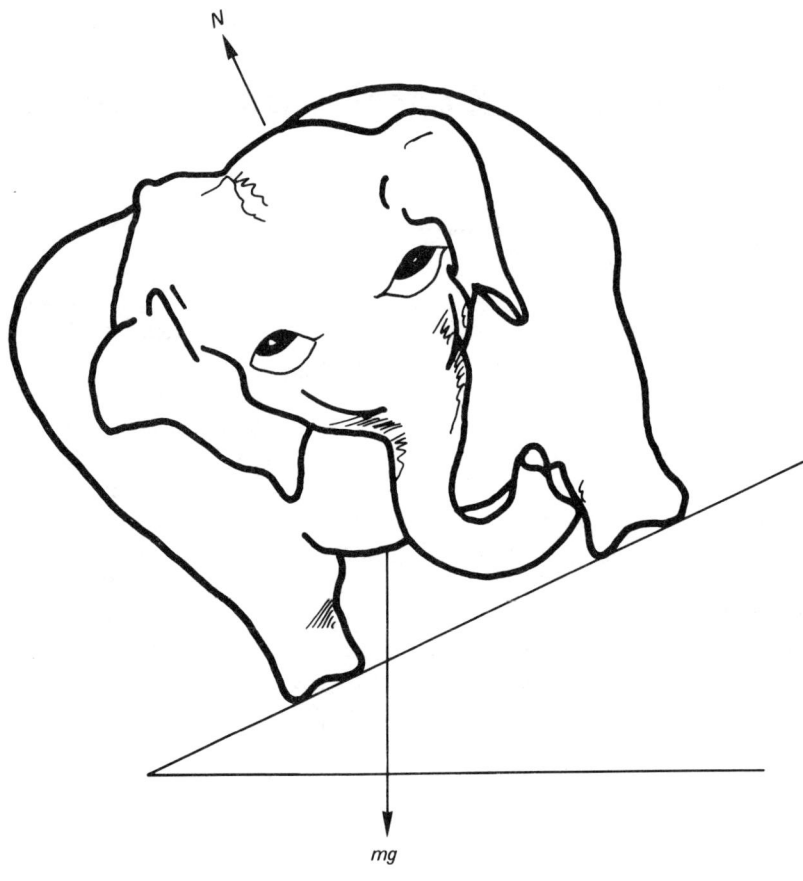

Figure 1.2 The real elephant

Once despised as a last resort for the solution of problems where 'exact' methods had failed, 'numerical' techniques are now at the forefront of every kind of scientific research — including mathematics itself. Thanks to the computer we shall be able to look at real practical problems, making only those concessions that are actually required by the numerical technique (that of 'finite differences') we shall use and by the time available to us. Figure 1.3 shows how we might well have to idealise the elephant: it is the 'finite-difference elephant' — a sort of cave-painting of the 1980s.

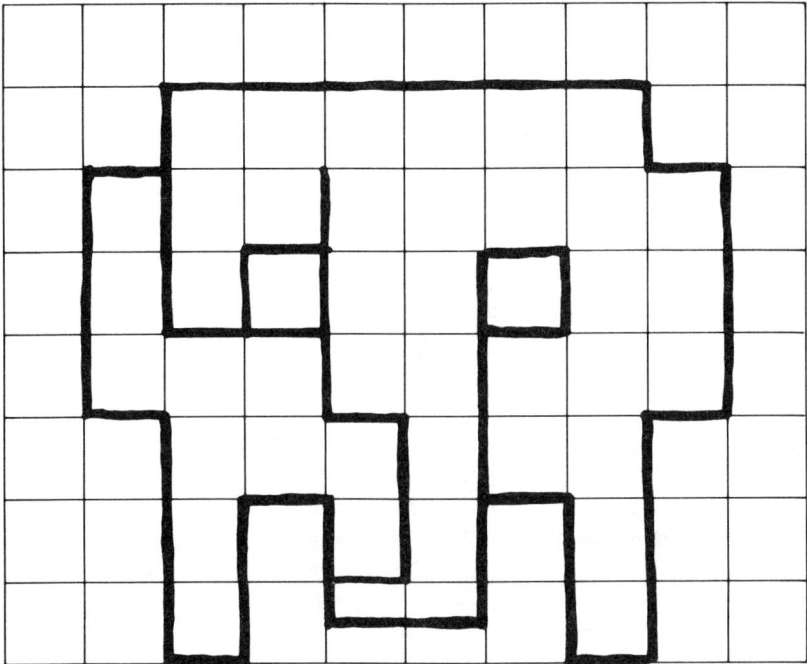

Figure 1.3 The finite-difference elephant

1.2 The Problems We Shall Solve

You will — especially if you are an undergraduate in science or engineering — by now have spotted that the vast majority of real-life physical phenomena are apparently governed by laws which boil down to second-order differential equations. This is not a coincidence: things that move do so under the control of Newton's Laws of Motion (in which the second derivative appears as acceleration). Electrical phenomena are governed by Maxwell's equations which also lead to equations involving second derivatives at worst. Anything that diffuses — like heat or the momentum of a real fluid — is likewise going to be the subject of a second-order differential equation.

It is clear that anyone who can solve second-order differential equations is well on the way to becoming a good physicist/engineer/mathematician. This book will explain in detail one very powerful and quite general method of dealing with most second-order (partial) differential equations.

The equations we shall solve will be those that govern the conduction of heat, the distribution of electrical potential and the flow of fluids — a fairly comprehensive list. The ideas will be illustrated as far as possible by simple computer programs. The ideas contained in the simple programs will be put together by the end of the book into a single, quite large BASIC program which will be used to solve real practical problems.

1.3 The Computer Program

A computer is an essential part of this book — without it you really cannot expect to follow the examples. The programs are written in BASIC: the versions in the text are suitable for the IBM PC and (with the modifications shown) for the Apple II. If you understand the BASIC used by your machine — if it is neither an Apple nor an IBM — you should have no trouble translating the programs so that you can run them. As a rough guide, the main differences between the BASICs will be in the same areas as those between IBM BASIC and Applesoft: slight variations in string-handling and different ways of telling the computer to clear the screen and to draw a line joining two points.

To give you some idea of the amount of work involved in typing in the programs listed in this book, it took the author five hours to type them all in, translating into a new dialect of BASIC as he went. It may take you a bit longer because you are not so familiar with the content, but it is unlikely that you will be typing all the programs at one go. Be warned, though: distinguish carefully between I's and 1's, O's and 0's.

As far as possible we shall avoid any 'special' features of the BASIC that we are using. This will make the programs less flashy but it will make them much easier to use on different machines (the 'in' word for this is 'portability').

When we come to include graphics we shall have to use some of the special features of each machine. We shall try to keep them to a minimum by restricting ourselves to subroutines that

> clear the screen
> draw axes
> move the cursor
> draw a line joining two points
> 'join the dots' defined by $(X(1), Y(1)), (X(2), Y(2)), \ldots, (X(N), Y(N))$

Because some 'primitive' BASICs are still around, mostly on mainframes, we shall use only variable names like A, B, . . ., A0, A1, . . . and not ones like ALF: arrays will have single-letter names A(I), . . . and not AA(I) nor A1(I). Strings are given names like A$, not A1$ nor AA$. All reasonable BASICs allow the names that we use. An extra advantage of these restrictions is that there is no danger of our embedding 'keywords' in the variable names, especially as the keywords vary from machine to machine.

We shall not use ELSE or WHILE: these are not generally available. As far as possible we shall avoid using GOTO, so that the programs are easier to follow.

Introduction: What this Book is about 5

The only regular exception to this will occur when we have to use 'short' GOTOs to jump round a couple of lines: mostly because we are avoiding ELSE.

As a result of all this self-denial on our part, you may well feel that you can improve the elegance of the program on your particular machine. Please feel free to do so — at your own risk. Remember that you may need to go back to the 'bedrock' no-frills version given here when you want to make the modifications suggested in the book, or if you decide to move to another machine with a different BASIC.

To give you some idea of the portability of the programs, they started life on a PRIME 400 and migrated via PETs, Apple II's, Honeywell Multics and a Sharp PC1211 (with only 2K of memory) to the IBM PC. None of the moves required substantial changes to make the programs run.

We shall try as far as possible to stick to a single structure for our computer programs. That means that at the outset they will tend to be a little more cumbersome than necessary: against that, by the time we are about two chapters into the book, the programs will be much easier to read than if we had used a separate structure for each one. The same structure will serve for the quite intricate program we shall finish up with — several hundred lines long. It will be quite easy for you to follow because you will be used to the structure by then. If you are translating the programs into your own computer's BASIC, you will find it very handy to know what each part of the program is meant to do, and you will be able to test and (if necessary) debug each subroutine separately. That, anyway, is the theory!

Here is the structure of our program.

Program 0

```
1 REM MAIN PROGRAM SECTION: LINES 1-999
999 STOP

1000 REM SUBROUTINE FOR INITIALISATION
1999 RETURN

2000 REM SUBROUTINE FOR THE PHYSICAL PROPERTIES
2999 RETURN

3000 REM SUBROUTINE FOR SETTING BOUNDARY CONDITIONS
3999 RETURN

4000 REM SUBROUTINE FOR CALCULATING THE SOLUTION
4999 RETURN

5000 REM SUBROUTINE FOR PRINTING AND PLOTTING RESULTS
5999 RETURN

9000 REM SUBROUTINES FOR GRAPHICS AT 9100 ETC.
9999 RETURN
```

Type this program into your computer, making any necessary changes to suit your version of BASIC as you go. If you RUN it you should find that it does nothing. It will serve as a sort of template for all our programs from now on.

2 The Finite-difference Method

2.1 Finite-difference Methods

Consider the problem

$$\frac{dy}{dx} = 0 \qquad (2.1)$$

where $y = a$ when $x = 0$

We can of course integrate (2.1) as it stands. We get

$$y = \text{constant}$$

and so $y = a$ is the solution.

But if instead of (2.1) we had to solve

$$\frac{dy}{dx} = \exp(-x^2) \qquad (2.2)$$

where $y = 0$ when $x = 0$

then we should have a problem that is not just a little more difficult to solve analytically but which — although it looks not very different from (2.1) — is actually impossible to solve analytically.

We need a method that can be used to solve (2.1) and which can, without too much bother, be adapted to solve equation (2.2) and others like it.

Figure 2.1 shows a section of the real line, from $x = x_1$ to $x = x_N$ chopped into $(N - 1)$ segments. For simplicity, we can suppose the segments to be of equal length.

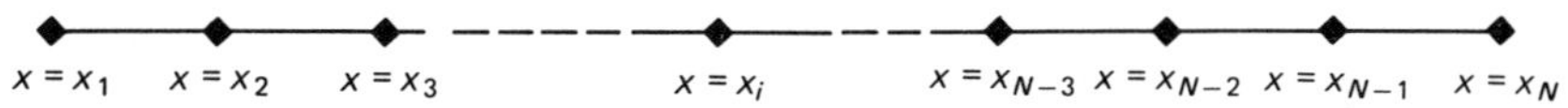

$x = x_1$ $x = x_2$ $x = x_3$ — — — $x = x_i$ — — $x = x_{N-3}$ $x = x_{N-2}$ $x = x_{N-1}$ $x = x_N$

Figure 2.1

Figure 2.2 shows the values of x, y at each of the points

$$x_1, x_2, \ldots, x_{i-1}, x_i, \ldots, x_N$$

together with the values of dy/dx at the points half-way between the nodes.

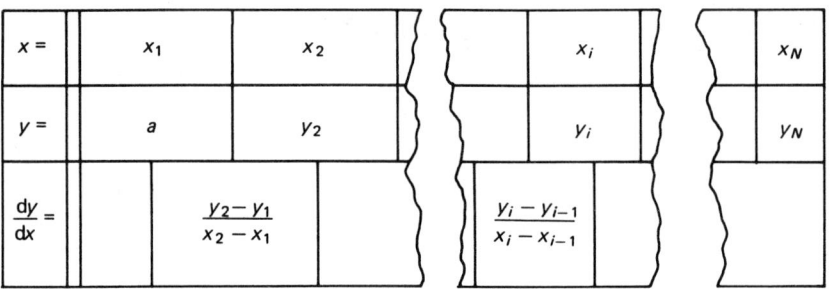

Figure 2.2

To calculate the value of dy/dx we have used the fact that

$$\frac{dy}{dx} = \frac{\text{increase in } y}{\text{increase in } x}$$

which will be nearly right if the increase in x is small enough.

There is a very useful theorem (the Mean Value Theorem) which says that a sufficiently well-behaved curve — and we can assume our curves to be well-behaved — will have a gradient somewhere between nodes $i-1$ and i exactly equal to

$$(y_i - y_{i-1})/(x_i - x_{i-1}) \qquad (2.3)$$

and we can see from figure 2.3 that this is no more than common sense. We can also see that for reasonably smooth curves the gradient is equal to expression (2.3) about half-way between the nodes.

If we now use the values in figure 2.2 for equation (2.1), we see that

$$\frac{y_i - y_{i-1}}{x_i - x_{i-1}} = 0$$

so that

$$y_i - y_{i-1} = 0$$

and

$$y_i = y_{i-1}$$

The values of y are therefore all the same, so that if $y = a$ when $x = 0$, then y must be equal to a everywhere.

The Finite-difference Method

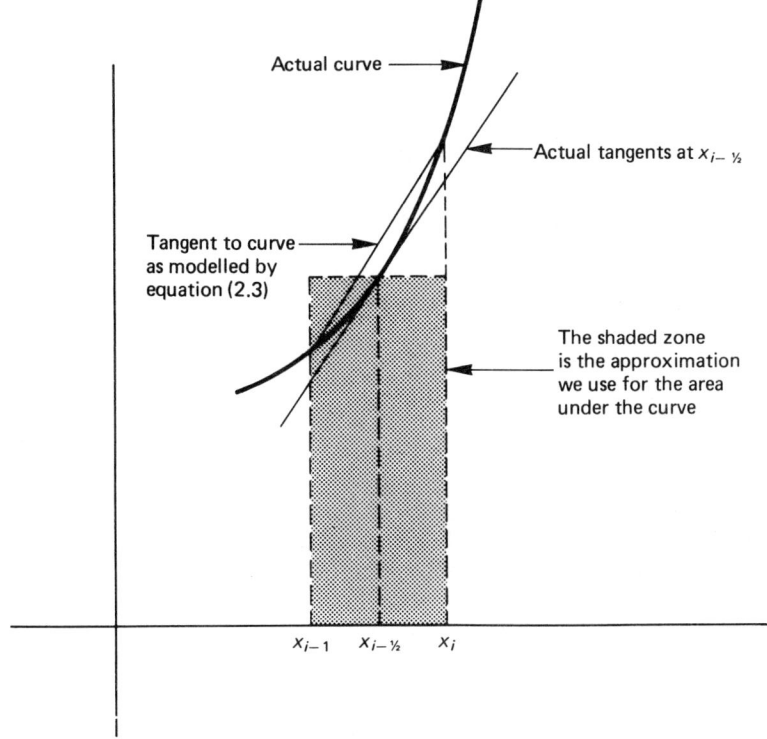

Figure 2.3

This very trivial problem shows that, here at least, the method — that of finite differences — works. It gives what we know to be the right answer

$$y = a$$

Now let us use the same method for solving equation (2.2). We get

$$\frac{y_i - y_{i-1}}{x_i - x_{i-1}} = \exp(-x_{i-½}^2)$$

or

$$y_i = y_{i-1} + (x_i - x_{i-1}) \exp(-x_{i-½}^2) \tag{2.4}$$

which you may recognise as the result of integrating equation (2.2) by working out the shaded area in figure 2.3.

Provided only that $x_i - x_{i-1}$ is small enough, equation (2.4) will give us accurate values of y. Starting at $x = 0$, we know that $y = 0$ there, and we can use equation (2.3) to generate a succession of values of y as we move to the right along the real line.

This, then, is the essence of the method of 'finite differences'. Figure 2.1 illustrates what we shall call the 'grid'. The points x_i are the 'grid nodes'.

In general, the solution of a problem in m dimensions will require an m-dimensional grid. Such a problem will arise if there are m independent variables. In the problems we have looked at so far, there has been only one independent variable (x) and one dependent variable (y): that is why we needed only a one-dimensional grid, as in figure 2.1.

Program 1
(Suitable as listed for the IBM PC or the Apple II).

Now let us write a short BASIC program that will solve equations like (2.2). We shall, of course stick to the structure of the 'template' Program 0.

First, we need to set up the grid. For this we need an array, X. Let us allow, for the moment, up to 20 elements. The solutions at each point will be stored in the array Y, also with 20 elements. We also have to decide the length of the section of the real line along which we are solving the equation. Let us call this L. We can calculate the length of each interval DX; if we are using N (out of the maximum of 20) nodes, then there will be $(N - 1)$ intervals, each of length $L/(N - 1)$. The values of X(I) are then calculated (line 100).

Next we set up a function to be the right-hand side of the equation. Let us call it FNA(X) (line 200).

We must decide on the boundary conditions (line 300).

Next we calculate the values of y, using equation (2.4). Note that we have to evaluate FNA(X) at the point mid-way between $X(I - 1)$ and X(I) (line 400).

Finally we arrange for the results to be printed out (line 500), and the program will STOP at line 999.

```
1 REM MAIN PROGRAM SECTION: LINES 1-999
100 GOSUB 1000: REM INITIALISE
200 GOSUB 2000: REM PHYSICAL PROPERTIES
300 GOSUB 3000: REM BOUNDARY CONDITIONS
400 GOSUB 4000: REM SOLVE THE PROBLEM
500 GOSUB 5000: REM PRINT THE SOLUTION
999 STOP

1000 REM SUBROUTINE FOR INITIALISATION
    1010 DIM X(20),Y(20)
    1020 N=11: REM NUMBER OF NODES
    1030 L=2: REM LENGTH OF LINE
    1040 DX=L/(N-1): REM INTERVAL BETWEEN NODES
    1050 REM CALCULATE THE GRID
    1060 X(1)=0
    1070 FOR I=2 TO N
    1080 X(I)=X(I-1)+DX
    1090 NEXT I
1999 RETURN
```

The Finite-difference Method

```
2000 REM SUBROUTINE FOR THE PHYSICAL PROPERTIES
   2010 DEF FNA(X)=EXP(-X*X)
2999 RETURN
3000 REM SUBROUTINE FOR SETTING BOUNDARY CONDITIONS
   3010 Y(1)=0
3999 RETURN

4000 REM SUBROUTINE FOR CALCULATING THE SOLUTION
   4010 REM CALCULATE THE Y'S
   4020 FOR I=2 TO N
   4030 Y(I)=Y(I-1)+(X(I)-X(I-1))*FNA((X(I)+X(I-1))/2)
   4040 NEXT I
4999 RETURN

5000 REM SUBROUTINE FOR PRINTING AND PLOTTING RESULTS
   5002 PRINT: PRINT "X","Y":PRINT
   5010 FOR I=1 TO N
   5020 PRINT X(I),Y(I)
   5030 NEXT I
5999 RETURN

9000 REM SUBROUTINES FOR GRAPHICS AT 9100 ETC.
9999 RETURN
```

This program is not particularly efficient but it is very simple and it works. The technique we have used is very similar to the one called 'Euler's method'.

If we RUN the program, we get the following output

X	Y
0	0
.2	.198009967
.4	.380796204
.6	.536556361
.8	.659081639
1	.748053252
1.2	.807692708
1.4	.844596613
1.6	.865676458
1.8	.876791701
2	.88220207

As we do not know the solution of equation (2.2), we have no immediate way of checking these results for accuracy. To check the program, let us solve an equation of which we know the solution

$dy/dx = \cos x$
with $y = 0$ when $x = 0$

Microcomputer Modelling by Finite Differences

We know the solution of this equation to be sin x. By modifying certain lines as follows

```
1020 N=17
1030 L=3.14159265
2010 DEF FNA(X)=COS(X)
```

and then RUNning the program, we get the following results

X	Y
0	0
.196349541	.195404064
.392699081	.383298859
.589048622	.556463694
.785398162	.708243942
.981747703	.832806772
1.17809724	.925365305
1.37444678	.982362568
1.57079633	1.00160819
1.76714587	.982362569
1.96349541	.925365306
2.15984495	.832806773
2.35619449	.708243944
2.55254403	.556463697
2.74889357	.383298862
2.94524311	.195404067
3.14159265	3.09364623E-09

and we can see that the program (and the method) work quite well. For example, the value of SIN(PI/4) should actually be 0.7071 ... while the program gives it as 0.7082. SIN(PI/2) is given as 1.0016 ... instead of 1.0000 — not too bad.

Exercise 2.1

Solve the equation $dy/dx = \sin x$, using Program 1, with $y = 0$ when $x = 0$, over the range $x = 0$ to $x = 2$. Modify line 1030 accordingly.

If you use 11 nodes (line 1020), you should get a solution

X	Y
0	0
.2	.0199666833
.4	.0790707247
.6	.174955832
.8	.30379937
1	.460464752
1.2	.638706224
1.4	.831417861
1.6	1.03091686
1.8	1.22924982
2	1.41850984

Check the accuracy of this solution by comparing it with what you get by integrating $dy/dx = \sin x$ and imposing the condition that $y = 0$ when $x = 0$.

Now see how the results change if you use 17 nodes. You should get, for example

1   .459997113

This value should be within 0.0003 of the result you got by integration — remember that the 'argument' 1 is radians, not degrees.

2.2 Second-order Problems

Consider the problem

$$\frac{d^2y}{dx^2} = f(x) \qquad (2.5)$$

where $y = 0$ when $x = 0$
and $y = 0$ when $x = L$

This problem is a 'second-order' one, because it includes mention of (at worst) second derivatives. However, the grid we use is again one-dimensional because there is only one independent variable (x). Figure 2.4 shows a close-up of the section of the grid surrounding the ith node. The points between the nodes are labelled in the obvious way, with the point $i + \frac{1}{2}$ lying mid-way between the node i and the node $i + 1$.

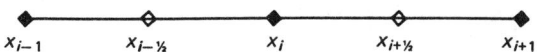

Figure 2.4

We shall use 'linear interpolation' except where we actually say that we are not doing so. This means that a quantity that varies from node to node will normally be assumed to do so uniformly. So the value of y, for example, at the point half-way between nodes i and $i + 1$ can safely be assumed to be half-way between the value of y at the node i and the value of y at node $i + 1$.

Now in order to solve equations like (2.5) we shall need to find an expression for the second derivative of y. We know that the second derivative is the rate of change of the first derivative; so

$$\frac{d^2y}{dx^2} = \frac{(dy/dx)_{i+\frac{1}{2}} - (dy/dx)_{i-\frac{1}{2}}}{x_{i+\frac{1}{2}} - x_{i-\frac{1}{2}}} \qquad (2.6)$$

We have already found the values of dy/dx at the points mid-way between the nodes: see expression (2.3). Now, writing out expression (2.6) in full, using (2.3), we get equation (2.7)

$$\frac{d^2y}{dx^2} = \frac{(y_{i+1} - y_i)/(x_{i+1} - x_i) - (y_i - y_{i-1})/(x_i - x_{i-1})}{(x_{i+1} - x_{i-1})/2} \qquad (2.7)$$

This, then, is the finite-difference model of a second derivative. It will serve us for the rest of this book.

The only precaution we need to take in order to make sure that the formulae we use are sufficiently close to reality for our purpose is to make the distance between the nodes i and $i + 1$ short enough. This is just an example of a notion that we take for granted most of the time.

Any curve you can draw, however sharply it bends, can be chopped into nearly straight segments if you chop it very small. The segments can be made as straight as you like, simply by chopping the curve up small enough.

This is a theorem that we use every day of our lives, without thinking. We use it, for example, whenever we read a street map. A street map sensibly ignores the curvature of the earth: from outer space the surface of the earth looks very curved indeed, but we are quite unaware of the earth's curvature because we live our lives on a tiny segment of the earth's surface. We should be crazy if we allowed for the curvature of the earth when we steered our cars or threw a ball.

For the moment, let us assume again that we can manage with a uniform grid, so that all the intervals between the nodes are equal to DX — as in Program 1. Then we have

$$x_i - x_{i-1} = \text{DX for } i = 2, 3, \ldots, N$$

and equation (2.5), which was our starting point, becomes (writing the value of y at the node i as Y(I))

$$Y(I + 1) - 2 * Y(I) + Y(I - 1) = \text{FNA}(X(I)) * \text{DX} * \text{DX}$$

or, in the form of a proper BASIC statement which also has the merit of expressing the quantity we are interested in (Y(I)) in terms of the other quantities

$$Y(I) = .5 * (Y(I + 1) + Y(I - 1) - \text{FNA}(X(I)) * \text{DX} * \text{DX}) \qquad (2.8)$$

The main difficulty with using equation (2.8) for Y(I) is that although it, like the expression (2.4) that we used for solving equation (2.2), refers to a quantity, Y(I − 1), which we should already know as we move from node I − 1 to node I along the grid, it *also* contains a reference to Y(I + 1) which we do *not* know at that stage.

One way round this is to use a technique that we shall often use in the rest of this book: that of *iteration*. Iteration consists simply of making a guess, using a formula (like (2.8)) to improve the guess, using the improved guess in the formula, . . . until (if it is successful) the guesses cease to improve — when we have a solution. The process is quite nicely illustrated by a flowchart (figure 2.5).

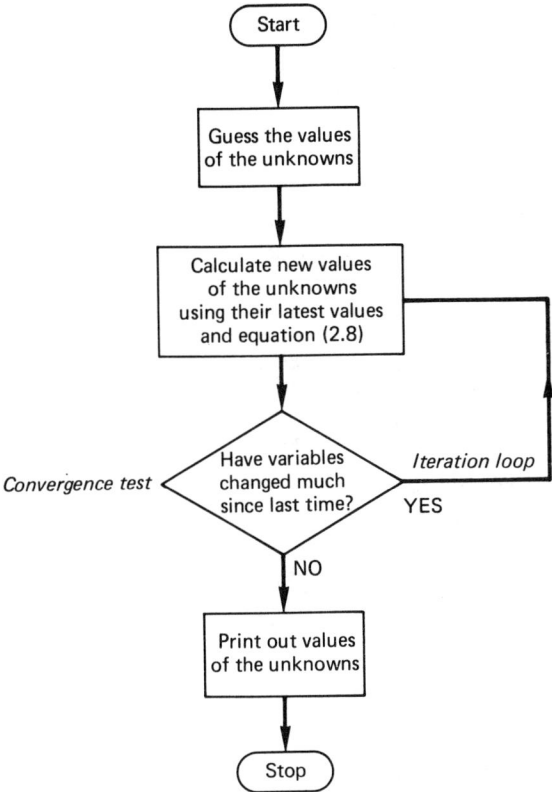

Figure 2.5

The test for whether the Y(I) have 'changed much since last time' will be performed by adding up the (absolute values of) the differences between the new and old Y(I)'s. If this 'residual' drops below, say, 1E−6 (that is, 0.000001) we shall say that the process has 'converged' to a result.

Another point to note is that while the right-hand side of (2.3) had to be calculated mid-way between the nodes, the corresponding quantity in (2.8) can be evaluated at the node. This is because the first and second derivatives are now being calculated at the node. Previously, the first derivative had to be calculated at the mid-way point, and so the right-hand side of the equation had to be calculated there too.

Program 2
(Suitable as listed for the IBM PC or the Apple II)

We can now write another program to solve equation (2.8), using mostly the same variables as Program 1, with the following additional variables

    D3 the 'residual' — a measure of the change
    C3 counter for the number of iterations
    O temporary store for old value of Y(I)

```
1 REM MAIN PROGRAM SECTION: LINES 1-999
100 GOSUB 1000: REM INITIALISE
200 GOSUB 2000: REM SET UP PROBLEM
300 GOSUB 3000: REM BOUNDARY CONDITIONS
400 GOSUB 4000: REM SOLVE THE PROBLEM
500 GOSUB 5000: REM PRINT THE SOLUTION
999 STOP
1000 REM SUBROUTINE FOR INITIALISATION
1010 DIM X(20),Y(20)
1020 N=11: REM NUMBER OF NODES
1030 L=2: REM LENGTH OF LINE
1040 DX=L/(N-1): REM INTERVAL BETWEEN NODES
1050 REM CALCULATE THE GRID
1060 X(1)=0
1070 FOR I=2 TO N
1080 X(I)=X(I-1)+DX
1090 NEXT I
   1100 C3=0: REM INITIALISE THE COUNTER C3
1999 RETURN

2000 REM SUBROUTINE FOR THE PHYSICAL PROPERTIES
   2010 DEF FNA(X)=2
2999 RETURN

3000 REM SUBROUTINE FOR SETTING BOUNDARY CONDITIONS
3010 Y(1)=0
   3020 Y(N)=0 : REM RIGHT BOUNDARY
3999 RETURN

4000 REM SUBROUTINE FOR CALCULATING THE SOLUTION
4010 REM CALCULATE THE Y'S
   4015 D3=0: REM SET RESIDUAL TO ZERO
   4020 FOR I=2 TO N-1 : REM ONLY TO N-1 NOW!!
   4025 O=Y(I): REM STORE PREVIOUS Y IN O
   4030 Y(I) = .5 * (Y(I + 1) + Y(I - 1) -  FNA(X(I))*DX*DX)
   4035 D3=D3+ABS(O-Y(I)): REM ACCUMULATE THE CHANGES
4040 NEXT I
   4100 C3=C3+1:  REM  INCREASE COUNTER
   4110  REM  PRINT OUT TYPICAL VALUE AND THE "RESIDUAL"
   4120  PRINT "RESIDUAL IS ";D3;" AFTER ";C3;" ITERATIONS"
   4130  PRINT "Y("; INT (N / 2);") = ";Y( INT (N / 2))
   4200  REM  IF NOT CONVERGED GO BACK TO 4015
   4210   IF D3 > 1E - 6 THEN GOTO 4015
4999 RETURN
```

The Finite-difference Method

```
5000 REM SUBROUTINE FOR PRINTING AND PLOTTING RESULTS
5002 PRINT: PRINT "X","Y":PRINT
5010 FOR I=1 TO N
5020 PRINT X(I),Y(I)
5030 NEXT I
5999 RETURN

9000 REM SUBROUTINES FOR GRAPHICS AT 9100 ETC.
9999 RETURN
```

The lines in Program 2 which did not appear in the same form (or at all) in Program 1 are indented to make it easy to identify the changes.

If you RUN this program, it will take 135 iterations to satisfy the rather strict convergence criterion D3 ⩽ 1E−6.

On the Apple II you will get output like this. (Because the Apple works to 9 significant figures and the IBM in single-precision to only 6 figures, we shall show Apple output: do not worry that the IBM gives 'wrong' answers if we look at numbers like 1E−7 − this makes no difference to the principle.)

```
RESIDUAL IS .64015625 AFTER 1 ITERATIONS
Y(5) = -.075
RESIDUAL IS .560625 AFTER 2 ITERATIONS
Y(5) = -.145
RESIDUAL IS .501513672 AFTER 3 ITERATIONS
Y(5) = -.210625
RESIDUAL IS .45288086 AFTER 4 ITERATIONS
Y(5) = -.2725
RESIDUAL IS .410998536 AFTER 5 ITERATIONS
Y(5) = -.331152344
```

and so on until the residual D3 drops below 1E−6 ...

```
RESIDUAL IS 1.13807619E-06 AFTER 133 ITERATIONS
Y(5) = -.959998304
RESIDUAL IS 1.02934428E-06 AFTER 134 ITERATIONS
Y(5) = -.959998467
RESIDUAL IS 9.31206159E-07 AFTER 135 ITERATIONS
Y(5) = -.959998613
```

```
X          Y

0          0
.2         -.359999476
.4         -.639999052
.6         -.83999876
.8         -.959998613
1          -.999998613
1.2        -.959998746
1.4        -.839998985
1.6        -.639999299
1.8        -.35999965
2          0
```

As we shall see in chapter 4, there is a neat way of avoiding iteration altogether for problems of this kind. For the moment, though, we shall be content to note that Program 2 does converge, to the correct result.

Exercise 2.2

Solve equation (2.4), with $f(x) = 2$, by integrating it. You should find that the results given by Program 2 are correct to 6 decimal places.

2.3 The General Second-order Problem

If we combine equations (2.2) and (2.4), add a term in y and introduce coefficients a, b and c, we get the second-order differential equation

$$a \frac{d^2y}{dx^2} + b \frac{dy}{dx} + cy = f(x) \tag{2.9}$$

We already have expression (2.5) for d^2y/dx^2. If we assume, for simplicity and for the time being, that we have a uniform grid — that is, that DX is constant, we get the simpler form

$$\frac{d^2y}{dx^2} = \frac{y_{i+1} - 2y_i + y_{i-1}}{dx^2}$$

We also need an expression for dy/dx. We must be careful to calculate dy/dx at the same point — that is, at the node — as the second derivative. As we already use the values $Y(I + 1)$ and $Y(I - 1)$ to calculate the second derivative, we might as well use them to get the first derivative. The obvious way of doing this is to write dy/dx as

$$\frac{Y(I + 1) - Y(I - 1)}{2 \, DX}$$

Equation (2.9) becomes

```
A*(Y(I+1)-2*Y(I)+Y(I-1))/DX/DX + B*(Y(I+1)-Y(I-1))/2/DX + C*Y(I)
  = FNA(X(I))
```

(*Note:* this is not a BASIC statement but an equation that we have to solve.)
This can now be put into the form of an expression for Y(I) in terms of

    Y(I − 1)
    Y(I + 1)
    A, B and C
    FNA (X(I))

The Finite-difference Method

We have

$$Y(I) = (G1*Y(I+1) + G2*Y(I-1) + G3)/G4 \qquad (2.10)$$

where

G1 = -A/DX/DX - B/2/DX

G2 = -A/DX/DX + B/2/DX

G3 = FNA(X(I))

G4 = C - 2*A/DX/DX

One very important point to note is that equation (2.10) is actually effectively the same as equation (2.8). This means that the computer program for solving (2.10) will be much the same as that for equation (2.8).

To make the program easier to use, we modify it further, to allow input of the values of A, B, C, N, Y(1), L and Y(N). It is now a fully interactive program which can be used to solve interesting problems.

Program 3

```
1 REM MAIN PROGRAM SECTION: LINES 1-999
100 GOSUB 1000: REM INITIALISE
200 GOSUB 2000: REM SET UP PROBLEM
300 GOSUB 3000: REM BOUNDARY CONDITIONS
400 GOSUB 4000: REM SOLVE THE PROBLEM
500 GOSUB 5000: REM PRINT THE SOLUTION
999 STOP

1000 REM SUBROUTINE FOR INITIALISATION
1010 DIM X(20),Y(20)
   1020 INPUT "NUMBER OF NODES ";N
   1030 INPUT "LENGTH OF DOMAIN ";L
1040 DX=L/(N-1): REM INTERVAL BETWEEN NODES
1050 REM CALCULATE THE GRID
1060 X(1)=0
1070 FOR I=2 TO N
1080 X(I)=X(I-1)+DX
1090 NEXT I
1100 C3=0: REM INITIALISE THE COUNTER C3
1999 RETURN

2000 REM SUBROUTINE FOR THE PHYSICAL PROPERTIES
2010 DEF FNA(X)=2
   2020 INPUT "ENTER A ";A
   2030 INPUT "ENTER B ";B
   2040 INPUT "ENTER C ";C
   2100  REM    CALCULATE G1, G2 AND G4
```

```
    2110 G1 =  - B / 2 / DX - A / DX / DX
    2120 G2 = B / 2 / DX - A / DX / DX
    2130 G4 = C - 2 * A / DX / DX
2999 RETURN

3000 REM SUBROUTINE FOR SETTING BOUNDARY CONDITIONS
    3010 INPUT "Y(1) ";Y(1)
    3020 PRINT "VALUE OF Y AT X=";L;
    3030 INPUT Y(N)
3999 RETURN

4000 REM SUBROUTINE FOR CALCULATING THE SOLUTION
4010 REM CALCULATE THE Y'S
4015 D3=0: REM SET RESIDUAL TO ZERO
4020 FOR I=2 TO N-1 : REM ONLY TO N-1 NOW!!
    4022 G3 = FNA(X(I)) : REM G3 RECALCULATED AT EACH NODE
4025 O=Y(I): REM STORE PREVIOUS Y IN O
    4030 Y(I) = (G1 * Y(I + 1) + G2 * Y(I - 1) + G3) / G4
4035 D3=D3+ABS(O-Y(I)): REM ACCUMULATE THE CHANGES
4040 NEXT I
4100 C3=C3+1: REM   INCREASE COUNTER
4110   REM  PRINT OUT TYPICAL VALUE AND THE "RESIDUAL"
4120   PRINT "RESIDUAL IS ";D3;" AFTER ";C3;" ITERATIONS"
4130   PRINT "Y("; INT (N / 2);") = ";Y( INT (N / 2))
4200   REM  IF NOT CONVERGED GO BACK TO 4015
4210   IF D3 > 1E - 6 THEN GOTO 4015
4999 RETURN

5000 REM SUBROUTINE FOR PRINTING AND PLOTTING RESULTS
5005 PRINT "X","Y",:PRINT
5010 FOR I=1 TO N
5020 PRINT X(I),Y(I)
5030 NEXT I
5999 RETURN

9000 REM SUBROUTINES FOR GRAPHICS AT 9100 ETC.
9999 RETURN
```

Once again we have indented new or modified lines to make them stand out. The values of G1, G2 and G4 can be calculated once for all at 2110-2130 but the value of G3 has to be calculated at each node, so it must appear inside the loop, at 4022. This is, of course, because G3 — unlike the other coefficients — is a function of X(I) and will vary along the grid.

Exercise 2.3

By setting N = 11, A = 1, B = 0 and C = 0, L = 2, Y(1) = 0 and Y(N) = 0, we should be able to reproduce the results of Program 2. Check that this is the case.

2.4 Graphics

From the outset in Program 0 we provided for the possibility of drawing graphs by including the subroutine at 9000. The following routine will enable us to draw graphs of the results of any output our programs produce. The routines are, of course, written for the high-resolution graphics of the IBM PC or the Apple, but it should not be too hard to translate them into any other form of BASIC, using the same variables. There are only small changes in lines up to 4999 but the routine at 5000 has had to be improved to provide an 'interface' between the simple numerical output we had before and the graphic routines in lines 9000-9999.

Program 4
(Suitable as listed for the IBM PC. The minor modifications needed for the Apple II are indicated in REM statements from line 9000 onwards)

```
100   GOSUB 1000: REM   INITIALISE
200   GOSUB 2000: REM   SET UP PROBLEM
300   GOSUB 3000: REM   BOUNDARY CONDITIONS
400   GOSUB 4000: REM   SOLVE THE PROBLEM
500   GOSUB 5000: REM   PRINT THE SOLUTION
999   STOP
1000  REM   SUBROUTINE FOR INITIALISATION
1010  DIM X(20),Y(20)
1020  INPUT "NUMBER OF NODES ";N
1030  INPUT "LENGTH OF DOMAIN ";L
1040  DX = L / (N - 1): REM   INTERVAL BETWEEN NODES
1050  REM   CALCULATE THE GRID
1060  X(1) = 0
1070  FOR I = 2 TO N
1080  X(I) = X(I -1) + DX
1090  NEXT I
1100  C3 = 0: REM   INITIALISE THE COUNTER C3
1999  RETURN

2000  REM   SUBROUTINE FOR THE PHYSICAL PROPERTIES
2010  DEF   FN A(X) = 2
2020  INPUT "ENTER A ";A
2030  INPUT "ENTER B ";B
2040  INPUT "ENTER C ";C
2100  REM     CALCULATE G1,G2 AND G4
2110  G1 =  - B / 2 / DX - A / DX / DX
2120  G2 = B / 2 / DX - A / DX / DX
2130  G4 = C - 2 * A / DX / DX
2999  RETURN

3000  REM   SUBROUTINE FOR SETTING BOUNDARY CONDITIONS
3010  INPUT "Y(1) ";Y(1)
3020  PRINT "VALUE OF Y AT X=";L;
3030  INPUT Y(N)
3999  RETURN
```

```
4000   REM   SUBROUTINE FOR CALCULATING THE SOLUTION
4010   REM   CALCULATE THE Y'S
4015   D3 = 0: REM   SET RESIDUAL TO ZERO
4020   FOR I = 2 TO N - 1: REM   ONLY TO N-1 NOW!!
4022   G3 =   FN A(X(I)): REM   G3 RECALCULATED AT EACH NODE
4025   O = Y(I): REM   STORE PREVIOUS Y IN O
4030   Y(I) = (G1 * Y(I + 1) + G2 * Y(I - 1) + G3) / G4
4035   D3 = D3 +  ABS (O - Y(I)): REM   ACCUMULATE THE CHANGES
4040   NEXT I
4100   C3 = C3 + 1: REM    INCREASE COUNTER
4110   REM    PRINT OUT TYPICAL VALUE AND THE "RESIDUAL"
4120   PRINT "RESIDUAL IS ";D3;" AFTER ";C3;" ITERATIONS"
4130   PRINT "Y("; INT (N / 2);") = ";Y( INT (N / 2))
4200   REM    IF NOT CONVERGED GO BACK TO 4015
4210   IF D3 > 1E - 6 THEN   GOTO 4015
   4300   PRINT "HIT RETURN TO CONTINUE"
   4310   INPUT Q$: REM APPLE WORKS BETTER WITH "GET Q$"
4999   RETURN


5000   REM   SUBROUTINE FOR PRINTING AND PLOTTING RESULTS
5002   PRINT: PRINT "X","Y":  PRINT
5010   FOR I = 1 TO N
5020   PRINT X(I),Y(I)
5030   NEXT I
   5300   PRINT "HIT RETURN TO CONTINUE"
   5310   INPUT Q$: REM APPLE WORKS BETTER WITH "GET Q$"
   5320   GOSUB 9100
   5400   REM   DETERMINE X1
   5410 X1 = X(1)
   5420   REM   DETERMINE X2
   5430 X2 = X(N)
   5440   REM   DETERMINE Y1 AND Y2
   5450 Y1 = Y(1)
   5460 Y2 = Y(1)
   5470   FOR I = 2 TO N
   5480   IF Y(I) < Y1 THEN Y1 = Y(I)
   5490   IF Y(I) > Y2 THEN Y2 = Y(I)
   5500   NEXT I
   5510 D6 = N
   5520   GOSUB 9800
   5530 D0 = 0
   5532 IF Y1>0 THEN D0=Y1
   5534 IF Y2<0 THEN D0=Y2
   5540 D1 = X1
   5545 D2 = X2
   5550 D7 = 10
   5560   GOSUB 9200
   5570 D0 = 0
   5572 IF X1>0 THEN D0=X1
   5574 IF X2<0 THEN D0=X2
   5580 D1 = Y1
   5585 D2 = Y2
   5590   GOSUB 9300
5999   RETURN
```

```
9000 REM subroutines for graphics at 9100 etc
9100 CLS:REM clear screen, apple hgr2 does this anyway
9110 SCREEN 2,,0,0: REM for apple use "HGR2"
9115 REM for apple use hcolor=3 to give white on black
9116 X8=640:Y8=200:REM X8,Y8 are screen dot-densities
9118 REM for apple x8=280, y8=192
9120 DEF FNX(X)=INT((X-X1)/(X2-X1)*(X8-1)+.5)
9130 DEF FNY(Y)=Y8-1-INT((Y-Y1)/(Y2-Y1)*(Y8-1)+.5)
9135 REM x1,y1 lowest values, x2,y2 highest values plotted
9199 RETURN
9200 REM draw an x-axis at y=d0 from x=d1 to x=d2
9205 X4=FNX(D1):Y4=FNY(D0):X5=FNX(D2)
9210 LINE (X4,Y4)-(X5,Y4):REM apple HPLOT X4,Y4 TO X5,Y4
9214 REM d7 notches
9216 S8=1
9218 IF Y4<5 THEN S8=-1
9220 FOR I=0 TO D7
9222 X6=X4+I/D7*(X5-X4)
9224 LINE (X6,Y4)-(X6,Y4-4*S8):REM apple uses hplot
9240 NEXT I
9249 RETURN
9300 REM draw a y-axis at x=d0 from y=d1 to y=d2
9305 Y4=FNY(D1):X4=FNX(D0):Y5=FNY(D2)
9310 LINE (X4,Y4)-(X4,Y5):REM apple uses HPLOT
9314 REM d7 notches
9316 S8=1
9320 FOR I=0 TO D7
9322 Y6=Y4+I/D7*(Y5-Y4)
9324 LINE(X4,Y6)-(X4+4*S8,Y6):REM apple uses HPLOT
9340 NEXT I
9349 RETURN


9400 REM move the cursor
9410 X7=X:Y7=Y
9449 RETURN
9500 REM draw a line to new (x,y)
9510 LINE(FNX(X7),FNY(Y7))-(FNX(X),FNY(Y)):REM apple uses HPLOT
9520 X7=X:Y7=Y
9599 RETURN
9800 REM join-the-dots routine
9805 REM array plotter for d6 points (x(i),y(i)), i=1 to d6-1
9810 FOR I=1 TO D6-1
9820 LINE(FNX(X(I)),FNY(Y(I)))-(FNX(X(I+1)),FNY(Y(I+1)))
9830 NEXT I
9840 X7=X(D6):Y7=Y(D6)
9899 RETURN
9999 RETURN
```

If you now RUN Program 4, setting N = 11, A = 1, B = 1, C = 1, N = 11, L = 1, Y(1) = 0, Y(N) = 1, you should see on your screen the graph shown in figure 2.6.

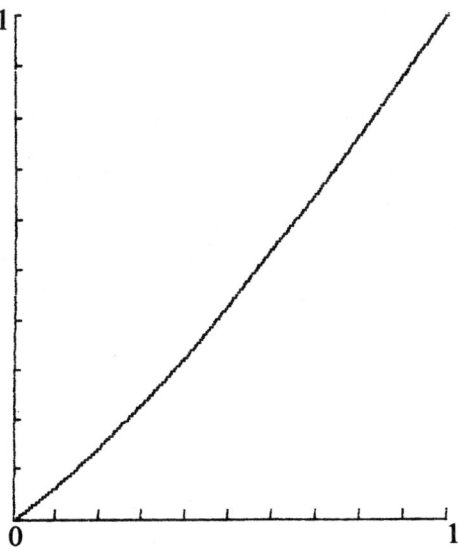

Figure 2.6

3 Convergence and Divergence

3.1 Convergence

So far we have assumed that, given long enough, the programs we use will get as close to 'the solution' as we care to specify. That is what we mean in this book by the word 'convergence': it is not quite the same as the meaning of 'convergence' in a maths book. When we need to distinguish between the rigorous idea of convergence in maths books and the rough-and-ready approach to convergence we shall use in our computer programs we shall refer to them respectively as

(i) true convergence, and
(ii) pseudo-convergence.

The classical definitions of convergence all involve phrases like 'for all n greater than N', which cannot form part of a computer algorithm of the kind we shall use. This is because we shall be making purely numerical tests and can do only a finite number of them. Computers may be fast but their speed is finite.

Our tests for convergence of an algorithm will at best be 'necessary' ones. None, however rigorous, is going to be 'sufficient' to ensure convergence. We can, for example, insist that

(i) the change in the dependent variable over one iteration cycle is smaller than some value we choose in advance, such as the value 1E−6 that we used in Program 4.
(ii) the number of iterations taken to satisfy (i) is reasonable in terms of the time we have to sit and wait for it to happen.

What we shall not be able to do is

(a) check that the same would have happened however small the value we had chosen: say 1E−9, or 1E−99, and so on
(b) check that once we had satisfied the test nothing would happen to make it fail (for the residual to rise again) if we had carried on iterating.

We are not likely to come up against examples that appear to satisfy a stringent test of type (i) but do not in fact converge. We shall look at such an example in section 3.3 below, just to remind ourselves that they exist.

It is of course essential to make sure that the 'changes' mentioned in test (i) are genuinely small ones.

Exercise 3.1

Try running Program 4 for $A = 1$, $B = 0$, $C = 0$, $L = 1$ and $FNF(X) = 2$, with $Y(1) = 0$ but with the value of $Y(N)$ set to 1000. Before doing this, find out where the RESET or BREAK button is on your computer. Why?

Exercise 3.1 should suggest to you that we ought really to be looking at fractional rather than absolute changes. In line 4035 of Program 4 we simply add up the absolute values of the differences between the old and the new values of the dependent variables at each node. This could be improved by replacing line 4035 by a line such as

```
4035 D3=D3 + ABS(O-Y(I))/ABS(O + 1E-6)
```

This change will ensure that the values of the residual are 'normalised' before we use them.

In this case, the effect of changing line 4035 is to make the program carry on for another five iterations. This is not too serious but in certain circumstances the program might go on for many more iterations, thereby wasting time, or for fewer iterations, losing accuracy.

Exercise 3.2

What is the point of adding 1E−6 to the denominator in line 4035? (Answer at the end of the chapter.)

Let us introduce a new variable

    CR   the convergence criterion

which we set as follows

```
1100 CR=1E-6
```

and use in line 4210

```
4210 IF D3>CR THEN GOTO 4015
```

Exercise 3.3

Determine the value of CR that will ensure that Program 4 with

    $N = 11$, $A = 1$, $B = 0$, $C = 0$, $FNF(X) = 2$, $L = 1$, $Y(0) = 0$, $Y(1) = 1$

will give answers correct to 4 places of decimals and then stop.

All this may seem very fussy, but if we had not made these changes, we might easily find that by making an apparently harmless alteration to the values of A,

Convergence and Divergence

B and C, we could produce 'results' that were little more than garbage. In fact, there are few better ways of

(i) wasting computer time on unnecessary iterations (by making CR too small) and/or
(ii) producing unconverged results and mistaking them for the answer (by making CR too big).

3.2 Divergence

After all the care we have taken to ensure that any results we get are truly converged, it may seem as though there is no need to worry about the danger of divergence. Far from it, alas. If we define 'divergence' as 'failure to achieve convergence in a reasonable time', we can recognise divergence by

(i) steady changes in the value of y (the dependent variable), suggesting that it is chugging off to infinity
(ii) wild fluctuations in y, or
(iii) oscillations in the value of y about a fixed value or about a value that is steadily changing.

The causes of divergence are legion but the most popular and widely used ones are

(a) lousy algorithms (like those in Programs 1, 2, 3 and 4 — but wait a chapter and all will be revealed)
(b) lousy programming (a real favourite)
(c) inherent difficulties in the problem, such as

    there just isn't a solution, or
    if there is a solution your method won't find it

    (these are happily rare in the kind of program we are going to look at)
(d) the accuracy of your computer or the fineness of your chosen mesh are not sufficient — you may be trawling for sardines with a mackerel net
(e) two solutions are so close that the computer cannot tell them apart — a special case of (d) in fact.

3.3 A Cautionary Tale

Suppose, knowing but little about convergence, we set out to sum the infinite series

$$S = 1 + \frac{1}{2} + \frac{1}{3} + \frac{1}{4} + \frac{1}{5} + \ldots + \frac{1}{n} + \ldots$$

and try to find out what the limit of S is as n tends to infinity. The kind of program we might write is given below.

Program 5
(Suitable as listed for the IBM PC or the Apple II)

```
100 S = 1
200    INPUT "NUMBER OF TERMS ";N
300    FOR I = 2 TO N
400 S = S + 1 / I
500    NEXT I
600    PRINT S
700    STOP
800    END
```

(This is a one-off program that does not conform to our template Program 0.)
If we run this program and

set   N=10   we get a sum of   2.92896825
             N=100   5.18737752
             N=1000   7.48547087
             N=10000   9.78760597

If we had the patience (about 2 hours) to set N = 1 000 000, we should get the sum of the first million reciprocals as 14.392 727 4.

Exercise 3.4

If, instead of telling the computer how many terms we wanted to add, we were to tell it to carry on until the answer stopped changing altogether, what would happen? Don't try to do this directly: think about it.
[A useful clue is this: try adding 1 and 1E−7 on your computer; then add 1 and 1E−8. Now add 1 and 1E−9. On most 8-bit machines, in BASIC, you should see that 1 + 1E−9 is 1. This is because the accuracy with which numbers are stored is sufficient to give 9 significant figures. (Not decimal places — the numbers are stored in 'scientific' form: 1.04E−2 rather than 0.0104. Try adding 1E−20 and 1E−28 and you should get the answer 1.00000001E−20.)]

Every machine has a limit to its accuracy, so that there is bound to come a point when no change occurs as a result of adding a term. So the computer is forced to conclude at that point that it has satisfied any convergence test you care to impose, however stringent.

But in fact the series is truly divergent! And we have shown that any computer program to compute it will pseudo-convergent.

If you want to convince yourself that the series truly diverges, chop it up into segments as follows

$$1 + \left(\frac{1}{2}\right) + \left(\frac{1}{3} + \frac{1}{4}\right) + \left(\frac{1}{5} + \frac{1}{6} + \frac{1}{7} + \frac{1}{8}\right) + \ldots$$

Each bracket has sum at least 0.5. There is an infinite number of them, so their sum is infinitely large.

Moral: Never ask a computer to do the impossible, because occasionally it will appear to succeed.

Exercise 3.5

The convergence test in line 4210 of Program 4 takes no account of the number of nodes we have used. Why should it?
[*Hint:* think about the accuracy of each term. When we test for (pseudo-)convergence we are testing the whole 'field' and not each node separately.]

Exercise 3.6

Plot the results we obtained for the sum of the harmonic series from Program 4 for various values of N on log–linear graph paper. More cheaply, especially if it would mean buying special graph paper, use ordinary squared paper and put each of the points 1EN (N = 1, 2, ..., 6) N units from the origin along the horizontal axis.

Given that ln (10) is 2.3026, show that the harmonic series behaves 'asymptotically' like in ln(N) (that is, that the graph of ln(N) and that of the sum appear to get closer as N gets larger).

3.4 Solving Systems of Linear Equations

In fact, Program 4 (like the earlier ones) is a scheme for solving systems of linear equations by iteration. The individual equations are all of the form of equation (2.8). We need to know if there is a general rule that will tell us whether our equations will (truly) converge.

Let us look at the simplest kind of simultaneous equations: two equations in two unknowns. We should be crazy to solve such a simple system by iteration when we know several direct and quick methods (such as substitution or elimination). But if we do solve them by iteration we find that, because we know what the result should be, we can see just what is happening when we use iteration — and just where it is liable to fail.

Let us take the equations

$$y = 2x + 1 \\ y = x \tag{3.1}$$

We have to choose one of them to be the equation for x and the other the equation for y: either

$$y = 2x + 1 \\ x = y \tag{3.2}$$

or

$$y = x$$
$$x = 0.5y - 0.5 \qquad (3.3)$$

Does it matter which of the schemes we choose? In fact it matters a great deal.

We can write a very simple program to compute the solution of two simultaneous equations

A1*X + B1*Y = C1

A2*X + B2*Y = C2 (3.4)

by the two possible iterative methods.

Program 6
(Suitable as listed for the IBM PC or the Apple II)
(Again, not in conformity with our template)

```
100   INPUT "A1:";A1
200   INPUT "B1:";B1
300   INPUT "C1:";C1
400   INPUT "A2:";A2
500   INPUT "B2:";B2
600   INPUT "C2:";C2
700   REM   BEGIN ITERATION 1
800   REM   USE EQUATION 1 FOR X, 2 FOR Y
850   PRINT "SCHEME 1": PRINT
860   PRINT "ITERATION";"   X"; TAB( 25);"Y"
900   FOR N = 1 TO 10
1000  X = (C1 - B1 * Y) / A1
1100  Y = (C2 - A2 * X) / B2
1200   PRINT N; TAB( 12);X; TAB( 25);Y
1300   NEXT N
1350   PRINT
1400  REM   BEGIN ITERATION 2
1500  REM   USE EQUATION 1 FOR Y, 2 FOR X
1520  X = 0:Y = 0: REM   RESET X,Y TO ZERO
1540   PRINT "SCHEME 2"
1550   FOR N = 1 TO 10
1600  Y = (C1 - A1 * X) / B1
1700  X = (C2 - B2 * Y) / A2
1800   PRINT N; TAB( 12);X; TAB( 25);Y
1900   NEXT N
```

When we RUN Program 6 with

$A1 = 2$
$B1 = -1$
$C1 = -1$

and

$$A2 = 1$$
$$B2 = -1$$
$$C2 = 0$$

we get the solutions of equations (3.1) and (3.2).

Scheme 1

ITERATION	X	Y
1	-.5	-.5
2	-.75	-.75
3	-.875	-.875
4	-.9375	-.9375
5	-.96875	-.96875
6	-.984375	-.984375
7	-.9921875	-.9921875
8	-.99609375	-.99609375

Scheme 2

1	1	1
2	3	3
3	7	7
4	15	15
5	31	31
6	63	63
7	127	127
8	255	255
9	511	511
10	1023	1023

Clearly the first scheme converges and the second diverges.

Exercise 3.7

By systematic experimentation with the values of A1, B1, ..., see if you can work out the rule for determining which scheme will converge and which will diverge. [You should find that the choice of C1 and C2 makes no difference but that the ratios of A1 to B1 and of A2 to B2 are crucial.]

It is possible to show that if we arrange the equations in the form

X = M1*Y + K1

Y = M2*X + K2

where both M1 and M2 are between −1 and +1, then the scheme we get will truly converge.

The result for two equations with two unknowns can be generalised to the case of n equations in n unknowns

$$x_1 = a_{12}x_2 + a_{13}x_3 + \ldots + a_{1n}x_n$$
$$x_2 = a_{21}x_1 + a_{23}x_3 + \ldots + a_{2n}x_n$$
$$\cdot$$
$$\cdot$$
$$\cdot$$
$$x_n = a_{n1}x_1 + a_{n2}x_2 + \ldots + a_{n-1,2}x_{n-1}$$

This scheme is convergent if the sum of the absolute values of the coefficients on the right-hand side of the equations is less than 1, except for perhaps one equation, in which the coefficients may add up to 1. This is known as the 'diagonal dominance criterion'. The proof that this condition is sufficient to ensure convergence is beyond the scope of this book.

Exercise 3.8

Use Program 6 to prove that the diagonal dominance criterion is not necessary for convergence. (In other words, find a pair of values for M1 and M2 in equation (3.5) that are not both between −1 and +1 but which give a (pseudo-)convergent sequence leading to the numerically correct solution.)

Answer to exercise 3.2

The idea behind adding 1E−6 to the denominator of the fraction in 4035 is to ensure that if all the values of Y happen to be zero (as they are at the outset in BASIC) 4035 will not give a 'DIVISION BY ZERO' error.

4 Better Solution Methods

4.1 The General Problem

We have been solving problems of the kind

$$g_4 y_i = g_1 y_{i+1} + g_2 y_{i-1} + g_3 \qquad (2.10)$$

The values of the g's will vary from one equation to the next. This means putting a subscript 'i' on them. For simplicity let us write

$$
\begin{array}{lll}
g_1 & \text{as} & c_i \\
g_2 & & a_i \\
g_3 & & -b_i \\
g_4 & & -d_i
\end{array}
$$

This will give us a set of N simultaneous equations

$$a_i y_{i-1} + d_i y_i + c_i y_{i+1} = b_i$$

that is, written out in full

$$
\begin{aligned}
d_1 y_1 + c_1 y_2 &= b_1 \\
a_2 y_1 + d_2 y_2 + c_2 y_3 &= b_2 \\
a_3 y_2 + d_3 y_3 + c_3 y_4 &= b_3 \\
&\vdots \\
a_{N-1} y_{N-2} + d_{N-1} y_{N-1} + c_{N-1} y_N &= b_{N-1} \\
a_N y_{N-1} + d_N y_N &= b_N
\end{aligned}
\qquad (4.1a)
$$

A system of equations like (4.1a) is known as a tri-diagonal system. It can be represented in matrix form by a tri-diagonal matrix system

$$
\begin{bmatrix}
d_1 & c_1 \\
d_2 & d_2 & c_2 \\
& a_3 & d_3 & c_3 \\
& & a_4 & d_4 & c_4 \\
& & & \cdots \\
& & & & a_{N-1} & d_{N-1} & c_{N-1} \\
& & & & & a_N & d_N
\end{bmatrix}
\begin{bmatrix}
y_1 \\ y_2 \\ y_3 \\ y_4 \\ \vdots \\ y_{N-1} \\ y_N
\end{bmatrix}
=
\begin{bmatrix}
b_1 \\ b_2 \\ b_3 \\ b_4 \\ \vdots \\ b_{N-1} \\ b_N
\end{bmatrix}
$$

But do not worry if you do not understand matrices: we did not really need to mention matrices except to explain the name of the algorithm in section 4.2, and we promise not to mention them again.

In fact, even if you do not know anything about matrices you can see why it is called tri-diagonal, because the main (top-left to bottom-right) diagonal is occupied, and so are the diagonals immediately above and below it. Everywhere else there are only zeros. This is not just chance: it is always the case for second-order equations, because the model

```
Y(I) = (G1*Y(I+1) +G2*Y(I-1) + G3)/G4
```
(2.10)

that we use for solving the problem will always relate the value of Y(I) to those of its immediate neighbours, Y(I + 1) and Y(I − 1).

Normally, what do we do when we are faced with a system of equations? We try to solve them by elimination or substitution — not by iteration, which we have been using so far in our program. And that is exactly what we shall try to do for these equations because they are tri-diagonal, which (as we shall see) allows us to substitute for each variable into the next equation. Just because there are a lot of equations and the coefficients become fiendishly complicated, that does not mean that we cannot solve them systematically. It will take a good deal of patience, but then patience is a quality that the computer has in abundance. So once again the computer is able to do something for us that we could do manually but which would actually be far too tedious and error-prone. Unlike us, the computer will never get bored: it may blow a fuse but even that happens quite rarely.

A set of equations like (4.1a) can, it turns out, be solved very efficiently and much more simply than we did in chapter 2 and in Programs 1-4.

4.2 The Algorithm — a Smart Trick

First let us write equations (4.1a) in a sort of semi-BASIC form

```
A(I)*Y(I-1) + D(I)*Y(I) + C(I)*Y(I+1) = B(I)
```

that is, written out in full

```
D(1)*Y(1)+C(1)*Y(2)                              =B(1)
A(2)*Y(1)+D(2)*Y(2)+C(2)*Y(3)                    =B(2)      (4.1b)
         A(3)*Y(2)+D(3)*Y(3)+C(3)*Y(4)           =B(3)
            ...
               ...
                  A(N-1)*Y(N-2)+D(N-1)*Y(N-1)+C(N-1)*Y(N)=B(N-1)
                              A(N)*Y(N-1)+ D(N)*Y(N)=B(N)
```

Better Solution Methods

We take the first of equations (4.1b) and solve it for Y(1)

$$Y(1) = B(1)/D(1) - C(1)/D(1) * Y(2) \tag{4.2}$$

If we use this expression for Y(1) and substitute into the second equation, we get

$$Y(2) = ((B(2)*D(1)-A(2)*B(1))/(D(1)*D(2)-A(2)*C(1))) \\ - Y(3) * C(2)*D(1)/ (D(1)*D(2)-A(2)*C(1)))$$

So, if we write

$$D(2) = (D(1)*D(2)-A(2)*C(1)) / D(1)$$

and

$$B(2) = (B(2)*D(1)-A(2)*B(1)) / D(1)$$

the equation for Y(2) becomes

$$Y(2) = B(2)/D(2) - Y(3) * C(2)/D(2) \tag{4.3}$$

If we use equation (4.3) and substitute into the third equation in (4.1b), we get

$$Y(3) = ((B(3)*D(2)-A(3)*B(2))/(D(2)*D(3)-A(3)*C(2))) \\ - Y(4) * C(3)*D(2)/ (D(2)*D(3)-A(3)*C(2)))$$

So, if we write

$$B(3) = (B(3)*D(2)-A(3)*B(2)) / D(2)$$

and

$$D(3) = (D(2)*D(3)-A(3)*C(2)) / D(2)$$

the equation for Y(3) becomes

$$Y(3) = B(3)/D(3) - Y(4) * C(3)/D(3) \tag{4.4}$$

and so on ... through the set of equations (4.1b). The only difference between the equations (4.2), (4.3) and (4.4) is the subscript. We can write them all as the system

$$B(I) = (B(I)*D(I-1)-A(I)*B(I-1)) / D(I-1)$$

and

```
D(I) = (D(I-1)*D(I)-A(I)*C(I-1)) / D(I-1)
```

or, more simply, if we cancel the $D(I-1)$'s

```
B(I) = B(I) - A(I)*B(I-1) / D(I-1)
```
(4.5a)

and

```
D(I) = D(I) - A(I)*C(I-1)) / D(I-1)
```
(4.5b)

We step through the system, replacing the B(I)'s and D(I)'s successively using these formulae (4.5).

The equation for Y(I) is

```
Y(I) = B(I)/D(I) - Y(I+1) * C(I)/D(I)
```
(4.6)

This means that if we know $Y(I + 1)$ we can find $Y(I)$, using the 'modified' coefficients B(I) and D(I). But we *do* know Y(N). So we can work out $Y(N-1)$, from which we can calculate $Y(N-2)$, and so on ... back down the system of equations (4.1b). This means that we can solve systems like (4.1b) without iteration. Brilliant!

The method is simple

(i) use formulae (4.5) to calculate new coefficients B(I) and D(I) from I = 2 to I = N − 1
(ii) use formula (4.6) to calculate the Y(I) from I = N − 1 down to 2 (known in the trade as 'back-substitution').

The whole scheme is called the *Thomas Algorithm* — sometimes the *Tri-Diagonal Matrix Algorithm* (TDMA).

4.3 The Program Revisited

To demonstrate just how effective the TDMA is, let us incorporate it into our Program 4 (5 and 6 were an interlude). Modifications required.

We shall need to store the coefficients A(I), B(I), C(I), D(I), replacing them as we modify them. These arrays are dimensioned in line 1015 and set in lines 4025–4040.

Next we shall calculate the modified B(I) and D(I) using equations (4.5): this happens in lines 4060–4080.

Better Solution Methods

In lines 4082-4095 we use equation (4.6) to give us the values of Y(I) for
I = N − 1, N − 2, ..., 2.

Finally, we have to make a slight adjustment, because the equations (4.1b) should not really include the first and last equations: the first node for which we can apply the equation is X(2), and the last node is X(N − 1), so we have

$$
\begin{aligned}
A(2)*Y(1)+D(2)*Y(2)+C(2)*Y(3) &= B(2) \\
A(3)*Y(2)+D(3)*Y(3)+C(3)*Y(4) &= B(3) \\
&\vdots \\
A(N-1)*Y(N-2)+D(N-1)*Y(N-1)+C(N-1)*Y(N) &= B(N-1)
\end{aligned}
\quad (4.7)
$$

Equations (4.7) are strictly tri-diagonal only if we move the terms involving Y(1) and Y(N) over to the right-hand side, which is where we keep our 'knowns'. This gives us

$$
\begin{aligned}
D(2)*Y(2)+C(2)*Y(3) &= B(2)-A(2)*Y(1) \\
A(3)*Y(2)+D(3)*Y(3)+C(3)*Y(4) &= B(3) \\
&\vdots \\
A(N-1)*Y(N-2)+D(N-1)*Y(N-1) &= B(N-1)-C(N-1)*Y(N)
\end{aligned}
\quad (4.8)
$$

So, if we are to incorporate all the information we have about Y(1) and Y(N), we must first modify the values of B(2) and B(N − 2) in agreement with the right-hand sides of equations (4.8). This is done in lines 4050 and 4055.

All of which gives us the next program.

Program 7
(Suitable as listed for the IBM PC or the Apple II)

```
100  GOSUB 1000: REM   INITIALISE
200  GOSUB 2000: REM   SET UP PROBLEM
300  GOSUB 3000: REM   BOUNDARY CONDITIONS
400  GOSUB 4000: REM   SOLVE THE PROBLEM
500  GOSUB 5000: REM   PRINT THE SOLUTION
999  STOP

1000 REM   SUBROUTINE FOR INITIALISATION
1010 DIM X(20),Y(20)
   1015 DIM A(20),B(20),C(20),D(20)
1020 INPUT "NUMBER OF NODES ";N
1030 INPUT "LENGTH OF DOMAIN ";L
1040 DX = L / (N - 1): REM   INTERVAL BETWEEN NODES
1050 REM   CALCULATE THE GRID
1060 X(1) = 0
1070 FOR I = 2 TO N
```

```
1080 X(I) = X(I - 1) + DX
1090 NEXT I
1100 C3 = 0: REM   INITIALISE THE COUNTER C3
1999 RETURN

2000 REM  SUBROUTINE FOR THE PHYSICAL PROPERTIES
2010 DEF  FN F(X) = 2
2020 INPUT "ENTER A ";A
2030 INPUT "ENTER B ";B
2040 INPUT "ENTER C ";C
2100 REM      CALCULATE G1,G2 AND G4
2110 G1 =  - B / 2 / DX - A / DX / DX
2120 G2 = B / 2 / DX - A / DX / DX
2130 G4 = C - 2 * A / DX / DX
2999 RETURN

3000 REM  SUBROUTINE FOR SETTING BOUNDARY CONDITIONS
3010 INPUT "Y(1) ";Y(1)
3020 PRINT "VALUE OF Y AT X=";L;
3030 INPUT Y(N)
3999 RETURN

4000 REM  SUBROUTINE FOR CALCULATING THE SOLUTION
4010 REM   CALCULATE THE Y'S
4015 D3 = 0: REM   SET RESIDUAL TO ZERO
4020 FOR I = 2 TO N - 1: REM   ONLY TO N-1 NOW!!
4022 G3 =   FN F(X(I)): REM  G3 RECALCULATED AT EACH NODE
   4025 A(I)=G2
   4030 B(I)=-G3
   4035 C(I)=G1
   4040 D(I)=-G4
   4045 NEXT I
   4050 B(2)=B(2)-A(2)*Y(1)
   4055 B(N-1)=B(N-1)-C(N-1)*Y(N)
   4060 FOR I=3 TO N-1
   4065 M1=A(I)/D(I-1)
   4070 D(I)=D(I)-M1*C(I-1)
   4075 B(I)=B(I)-M1*B(I-1)
   4080 NEXT I
   4082 Y(N-1)=B(N-1)/D(N-1)
   4084 FOR I=N-2 TO 2 STEP -1
   4086 O=Y(I)
   4088 Y(I)=(B(I)-C(I)*Y(I+1))/D(I)
   4090 D3=D3+ABS(O-Y(I))
   4095 NEXT I
4100 C3 = C3 + 1: REM    INCREASE COUNTER
4110 REM    PRINT OUT TYPICAL VALUE AND THE "RESIDUAL"
4120 PRINT "RESIDUAL IS ";D3;" AFTER ";C3;" ITERATIONS"
4130 PRINT "Y(";  INT  (N / 2);") = ";Y(  INT  (N / 2))
4200 REM    IF NOT CONVERGED GO BACK TO 4015
4210 IF D3 > 1E - 6 THEN   GOTO 4015
4300 PRINT "HIT RETURN TO CONTINUE"
4310 INPUT Q$: REM APPLE IS BETTER WITH "GET Q$"
4999 RETURN
```

Better Solution Methods

The remaining subroutines (5000-5999 and 9000-9999) are exactly as in Program 4.

If we RUN Program 7 for the same inputs as we used for Program 2, we get the same answers (actually we get very slightly better ones!) much more quickly. There is no actual need for iteration at all but the program does not 'know' that until it has been through a second iteration and there is a change of precisely zero. The results we get are as follows

```
RESIDUAL IS 6.24 AFTER 1 ITERATIONS
Y(5) = -.96
RESIDUAL IS 0 AFTER 2 ITERATIONS
Y(5) = -.96
HIT RETURN TO CONTINUE


X       Y

0       0
.2     -.36
.4     -.64
.6     -.84
.8     -.96
1      -1
1.2    -.96
1.4    -.84
1.6    -.64
1.8    -.36
2       0

HIT RETURN TO CONTINUE
```

and the graph should look like figure 4.1 below.

Exercises 4.1

Exercise 4.1.1. Solve the equation

$$\frac{d^2y}{dx^2} + 2\frac{dy}{dx} + y = \exp(-x^2)$$

with $y = 0$ at $x = 0$ and $y = 0$ at $x = 1$ using Program 7. You will have to modify line 2010 appropriately.

Exercise 4.1.2. Solve the equation

$$\frac{d^2y}{dx^2} + 2\frac{dy}{dx} + y = \exp(-x^2)$$

with $y = 0$ at $x = 0$ and $y = 0$ at $x = 5$ using Program 7. The graph you get will look rather odd and unsatisfactory. Can you suggest reasons and a cure (but do not try to implement your cure just yet)?

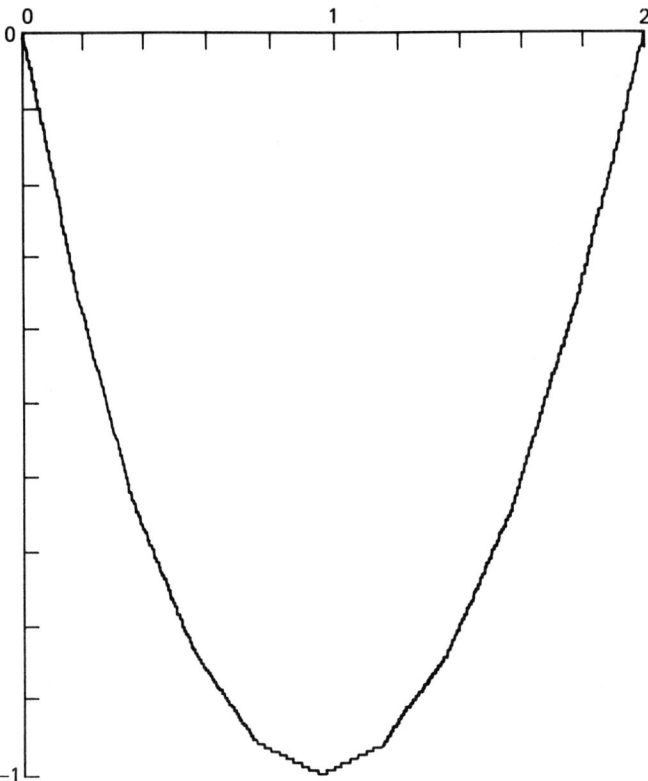

Figure 4.1

Exercise 4.1.3. Solve the equation

$$a \frac{d^2y}{dx^2} + b \frac{dy}{dx} + cy = \exp(-x^2)$$

with systematic variation in

(i) the boundary conditions for given coefficients
(ii) the coefficients for given boundary conditions.

4.4 A Neater Algorithm

By now you will have realised that using the TDMA saves most of the computing

Better Solution Methods

time needed for solving equations (4.1b) as compared with the method of Program 4. However, line 1015

```
1015 DIM A(20),B(20),C(20),D(20)
```

shows that for large problems we may encounter problems of storage, especially if we are using a pocket computer with, say, 2K of storage (no joke: the author has created versions of all the programs in this book for such a machine).

To get round this, let us look again at equations (4.5)

```
B(I) = B(I) - A(I)*B(I-1) / D(I-1)
```

and (4.5)

```
D(I) = D(I) - A(I)*C(I-1)) / D(I-1)
```

If we write

```
L(I-1) = C(I-1)/D(I-1)
M(I-1) = B(I-1)/D(I-1)
```
(4.9)

and let

```
D(I) = D(I) - A(I) * L(I-1)
B(I) = B(I) - A(I) * M(I-1)
```
(4.10)

together with

```
L(I) = C(I) / D(I)
M(I) = B(I) / D(I)
```

we see that the only (I − 1) terms, and thus the only ones that we need to store at this stage, are

```
L(I-1)   and   M(I-1)
```

When we come to the back-substitution stage

```
Y(I) = B(I)/D(I) - Y(I+1) * C(I)/D(I)
```
(4.6)

we now have

```
Y(I-1) = M(I-1) - L(I-1) * Y(I)
```
(4.11)

which shows that we still need only the $L(I-1)$ and $M(I-1)$, so that there is in fact no need to carry round all four of the A(I), B(I), C(I) and D(I): we need only two items of information, not four. Putting L(I) as C(I) and M(I) as B(I), we can write

```
1015 DIM B(20),C(20)
```

and

```
4025 A1=G2
4030 B(I)=-G3
4035 C(I)=G1
4040 D1=-G4
4045 NEXT I
4050 B(2)=B(2)-A1*Y(1)
4052 B(2)=B(2)/D1
4053 C(2)=C(2)/D1
4055 B(N-1)=B(N-1)-C(N-1)*Y(N)
4060 FOR I=3 TO N-1
4065 D=D1-A1*C(I-1)
4070 B(I)=(B(I)-A1*B(I-1))/D
4075 C(I)=C(I)/D
4080 NEXT I
4082 Y(N-1)=B(N-1)
4084 FOR I=N-2 TO 2 STEP -1
4086 O=Y(I)
4088 Y(I)=B(I)-C(I)*Y(I+1)
4090 D3=D3+ABS(O-Y(I))
4095 NEXT I
```

Using this chunk of program instead of the corresponding one in Program 7 should lead to exactly the same answers as before, while using fewer arrays.

Program 8
(Suitable as listed for the IBM PC or the Apple II)

As Program 7 but with modifications given above for lines 1015 and 4025-4095.

4.5 Gradient Boundary Conditions

So far we have assumed that we are given the values of the dependent variable (Y) at the boundaries. We have always been able to specify the values of Y(1) and Y(N). This will not necessarily be the case for all problems: very often we know not the values of Y at the edge but the value of dy/dx there. Of course, if we are to fix the values of Y uniquely everywhere, we shall need to know the value of Y at one point in the domain. That is just common sense: knowing only

Better Solution Methods

the slope of a road everywhere would not tell us its absolute height above sea level anywhere.

If we know the gradient at X(1), say, and not the value of Y(1), let us call the gradient G and we have

```
G = (Y(2) - Y(1))/DX
```

and hence

```
Y(1) = Y(2) - G*DX
```
(4.12)

We could modify Program 7 as follows

```
3010 INPUT "ENTER GRADIENT AT X(1) ";G

4048 Y(1) = Y(2) - G*DX
```

This, however, is a very bad way to solve the problem, because we need to know the value of Y(2) before we can start, and the value of Y(1) will be incorrect until the value of Y(2) is right — in other words we shall find our program iterating again. We shall have undone all the good work of the TDMA.

The trick is this: to avoid iterating we must always try to get the information into the coefficients, not the solutions: this is what we did before by modifying the coefficients and then using the modified coefficients for back-substitution. We can do the same here.

The equation for Y(1) is

```
A(2) * Y(1)  + D(2) * Y(2) + C(2) * Y(3)  =  B(2)
```

If we replace Y(1) using formula (4.12), we get

```
A(2) * (Y(2) - G * DX) + D(2) * Y(2) + C(2) * Y(3)  =  B(2)
```

or in other words

```
(D(2) + A(2)) * Y(2)  +  C(2) * Y(3)  =  B(2) + A(2) * G * DX
```

So, if we modify the coefficients as follows

```
4048   D(2) = D(2) + A(2)
4050   B(2) = B(2) + A(2) * G * DX
```

we shall have incorporated the information about the boundary at X(1) directly into the coefficients D(2) and B(2). There will be no iteration.

This last modification can be made only in Program 7 with the earlier version of the TDMA because D(2) and B(2) are treated differently in the later one: we could get round this.

In order that the graph should look right, we must supply a value (other than zero, which is what it will be as things are) for Y(1)

```
5005   Y(1) = Y(2) - G * DX
```

Program 9
(Suitable as listed for the IBM PC or the Apple II)

As Program 7 but with lines 3010, 4048, 4050 and 5005 modified as shown:

```
3010 INPUT "ENTER GRADIENT AT X(1) ";G

4048 D(2) = D(2) + A(2)
4050 B(2) = B(2) + A(2) * G * DX
5005 Y(1) = Y(2) - G * DX
```

5 Further Improvements

5.1 Non-constant Coefficients

There is nothing about our finite-difference method that assumes that the coefficients a, b and c in

$$a \frac{d^2y}{dx^2} + b \frac{dy}{dx} + cy = f(x) \tag{2.9}$$

have to be constant any more than the right-hand side has had to be. If the coefficients are just functions of x they will cause no extra problems. Of course, if they involve y or dy/dx they will cause the program to iterate again, and there is little we can do about that.

The values of the G's will have to be calculated at each node rather than once for all time at the outset. So we have to define functions FNA(X), FNB(X), FNC(X) in lines 2020-2040, removing the input of A, B and C. We also remove the calculation of the G's which must now be postponed to the subroutine at 4000.

We have set up the coefficients to solve the equation

$$\frac{d^2y}{dx^2} - 2x \frac{dy}{dx} + (x^2 + 2)y = \exp(x^2/2 + x)$$

The calculation of the G's is performed in lines 4022-4040.

Program 10
(Suitable as listed for the IBM PC or the Apple II)

```
2000 REM    SUBROUTINE FOR THE PHYSICAL PROPERTIES
2010 DEF    FN F(X) = EXP((X*X +2*X)/2)
  2020 DEF    FN A(X) = 1
  2030 DEF    FN B(X) = - 2 * X
  2040 DEF    FN C(X) = X * X + 2
2100 REM        CALCULATE G1,G2 AND G4
  2110 REM DO THIS IN SUBROUTINE AT 4000 LIKE G3
  2120 REM
  2130 REM
2999 RETURN

4000 REM. SUBROUTINE FOR CALCULATING THE SOLUTION
```

```
4010 REM   CALCULATE THE Y'S
4015 D3 = 0: REM   SET RESIDUAL TO ZERO
4020 FOR I = 2 TO N - 1: REM    ONLY TO N-1 NOW!!
   4022 A=FNA(X(I)):B=FNB(X(I)):C=FNC(X(I)): G3 =    FN F(X(I))
   4025 A(I)= B/2/DX - A/DX/DX
4030 B(I)=-G3
   4035 C(I)= -B/2/DX - A/DX/DX
   4040 D(I)= -C + 2*A/DX/DX
4045 NEXT I
4050 B(2)=B(2)-A(2)*Y(1)
4055 B(N-1)=B(N-1)-C(N-1)*Y(N)
4060 FOR I=3 TO N-1
4065 M1=A(I)/D(I-1)
4070 D(I)=D(I)-M1*C(I-1)
4075 B(I)=B(I)-M1*B(I-1)
4080 NEXT I
4082 Y(N-1)=B(N-1)/D(N-1)
4084 FOR I=N-2 TO 2 STEP -1
4086 O=Y(I)
4088 Y(I)=(B(I)-C(I)*Y(I+1))/D(I)
4090 D3=D3+ABS(O-Y(I))
4095 NEXT I
4100 C3 = C3 + 1: REM    INCREASE COUNTER
4110 REM   PRINT OUT TYPICAL VALUE AND THE "RESIDUAL"
4120 PRINT "RESIDUAL IS ";D3;" AFTER ";C3;" ITERATIONS"
4130 PRINT "Y("; INT (N / 2);") = ";Y( INT (N / 2))
4200 REM   IF NOT CONVERGED GO BACK TO 4015
4210 IF D3 > 1E - 6 THEN   GOTO 4015
4300 PRINT "HIT RETURN TO CONTINUE"
4310 INPUT Q$
4999 RETURN
```

All the other subroutines remain unchanged from Program 7.

5.2 Gradients at the Boundaries

From here on in this chapter we shall take a slightly more critical look at some of the ideas that we have been using and suggest improvements. We shall not actually implement the ideas in Program 7, simply because we are about to develop a much more ambitious program in which we shall try to include all our best ideas.

In chapter 4, when we introduced the idea of specifying the gradient rather than the value of Y at the boundary, we were forced to make do with the value of the gradient not in fact at the boundary but half-way between the boundary and the first node. In view of all the trouble that we are taking to get the answers as accurate as possible, this is just not good enough.

To get round the problem we introduce 'phantom nodes' $X(1)$ and $X(N)$, just outside the boundaries. The grid is designed so that the actual physical boundaries are exactly half-way between X(1) and X(2) at one end, and half-way between X(N − 1) and X(N) at the other end. Figure 5.1 shows the former arrangement and the new grid below it.

Now, of course, we can specify the gradient at the boundary at a point midway between the outermost nodes: in other words, remembering figure 2.3, just where our model gets the gradients most nearly right.

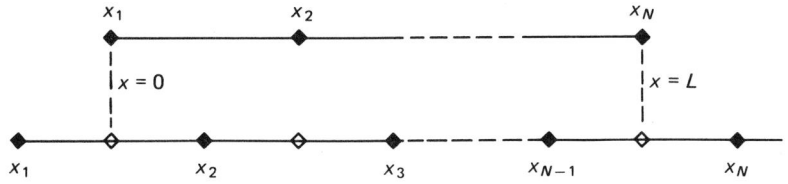

Figure 5.1

5.3 The Non-uniform Grid

Another problem we came up against in chapter 4 was that when we produced a really dramatic curve for the solution of exercise 4.1, the method was not quite up to producing smooth curves with the same number of nodes as had been adequate for the less curvy curves. The trouble is basically that in order to get enough grid nodes in the place where we need them − where everything interesting is happening − we have to put a lot of nodes in places where the curve is boringly straight. That applies, of course, only so long as we remain wedded to the notion of a uniform grid. The remedy is to write our solution procedure in such a way that it does not depend on the uniformity of the mesh. We can then sprinkle the nodes exactly where they will be most useful.

One handy device is to provide for a uniformly expanding or contracting grid which will allow us to bunch points at one end or other of the grid. Figure 5.2 shows such a grid, complete with its phantom points.

Figure 5.2

The problem is then as follows: given the number N of nodes, the width L of the body, the expansion factor F1 (the ratio of the width of each 'cell' to that of the cell on its left), what is the width DX of the first cell?

The solution is quite easy to find using the theory of geometric progressions. We have the equation

```
L=DX+F1*DX+(F1^2)*DX+...+(F1^(N-2))*DX-DX/2-(F1^(N-2))*DX/2
```

which gives

```
DX = 2*L*(1-F1) / (1+F1) / (1 - F1^(N-2))
```
(5.1)

Exercise 5.1

Derive equation (5.1).
 It is not a good idea to set F1 = 1.0 exactly in equation (5.1): why not?

Bear in mind, though, that equation (5.1) specifies just one example of a non-uniform grid — one that we happen to find useful in a lot of situations. The principle works just as well however you decide to specify your grid.

5.4 The Finite-difference Equations

If we no longer have a uniform grid for the solution of our equation

$$a \frac{d^2 y}{dx^2} + b \frac{dy}{dx} + cy = f(x) \tag{2.9}$$

we have to use

$$\frac{d^2 y}{dx^2} = \frac{(dy/dx)_{i+\frac{1}{2}} - (dy/dx)_{i-\frac{1}{2}}}{x_{i+\frac{1}{2}} - x_{i-\frac{1}{2}}} \tag{2.6}$$

We can obtain expressions G1, etc., to ensure that we can write

```
Y(I) = (G1*Y(I+1) + G2*Y(I-1) + G3)/G4
```
(2.10)

though we shall not be able to use the simple form

G1 = −A/DX/DX − B/2/DX
G2 = −A/DX/DX + B/2/DX
G4 = C − 2 * A/DX/DX

because we shall not have a single value of DX.

The only additional complications that would be introduced as a result of using a non-uniform grid are that all the DX's have to be replaced with functions of X(I). The values of X(I) are, of course, known, so that the expressions are just a little bit more cumbersome but the principle and the shape of the equations remain unchanged.

Exercise 5.2

Use Program 10 with 99 nodes, that is

```
1010 DIM X(99), Y(99)
1015 DIM A(99), B(99), C(99), D(99)
```

and

```
2010 DEF FN F(X) =0
```

to show that the solutions of

(a) $i'' + 3i' + i = 0; i = 0$ when $t = 0, i = 1\mathrm{E}{-}10$ when $t = 10$
(b) $i'' + 2i' + i = 0; i = 0$ when $t = 0, i = 1\mathrm{E}{-}10$ when $t = 10$
(c) $i'' + i' + i = 0; i = 0$ when $t = 0, i = 1\mathrm{E}{-}10$ when $t = 10$

give, respectively, the shapes of transient associated with

(a) overdamping
(b) critical damping
(c) underdamping (oscillation).

The 'primes' denote differentiation with respect to t. The computer program does not, of course, give a hoot whether the independent variable is called x or t or the dependent variable y or i. The transient solution is the one that occurs in the period after switching on a circuit (that is, from $i = 0, t = 0$ as in the examples).

With any luck, the solutions should look like figure 5.3 below.

Exercise 5.3

Use Program 9 with the same equations as in 5.1.1, but with the right-hand side set to $\sin(100 * \mathrm{PI} * \mathrm{T})$, that is

```
2010   DEF FN F(X) = SIN(314.159*X)
```

We can see the effect of a mains-frequency driving force. RUN the program in each case first with 20 nodes and then with 99 nodes. This will show just how important the sampling-rate is. You will find that you get strikingly different (and mostly wrong) solutions if you try to solve the problem over more than about 0.4 seconds (20 cycles) or with fewer than 5 nodes per cycle. This is, of course, because we are 'trawling for sardines with a mackerel net' as we feared in section 3.2: in this example, a great deal happens within each cell and we cannot hope to pick this up except by putting nodes there.

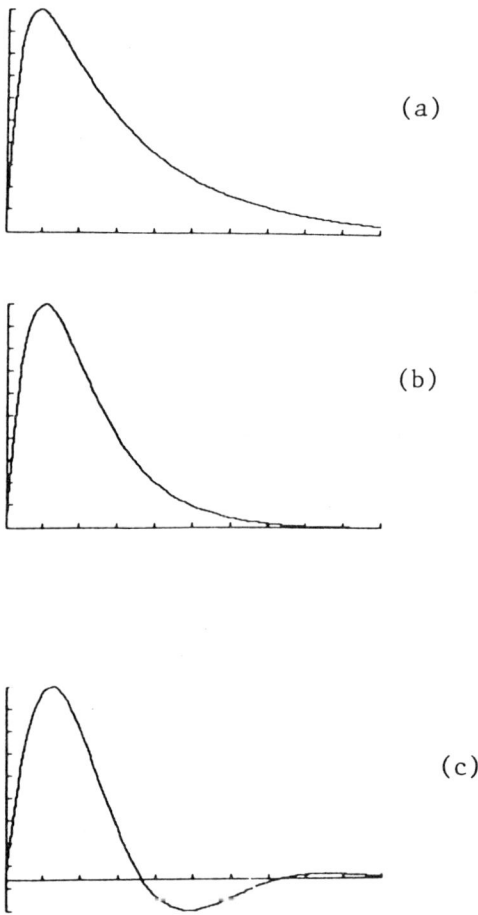

Figure 5.3

6 More Ambitious Applications: the Heat Equation

6.1 Background

We have written some quite useful programs for solving differential equations in one dimension (chapters 1-5). In fact the programs contain just about all the ideas needed for dealing with partial differential equations in two space dimensions: everything we have done so far will be useful in solving much more complicated problems. But that can wait till the next chapter: in this chapter we shall try to show how easily we can make the programs and notions of chapters 1-5 be of use in solving simple physical problems in one space dimension.

Mathematics is a very beautiful subject in its own right but for everyone except the serious, committed mathematician it takes off only when it has some relevance to the real world around us. The techniques we have developed in the first five chapters can be used to help us design a computer program that will solve problems in 'heat transfer', which is essentially the study of how things (bodies or fluids) heat up and cool down. The general idea is that we feed in numbers which tell us what size and shape the body or fluid is, what it is made of, what is around it, what is done to it (for example, heating it up from inside) and the initial temperatures everywhere in it: we get out numbers that tell us what the temperatures are everywhere at later times. Traditionally, the way of getting from the input to the output was by means of very tricky mathematics: now, using computers and the techniques of chapters 1-5, we can write a straightforward computer program to do the work for us.

The 'equation of heat conduction', with 'sources', for a body with 'thermal conductivity' k, is (using the shorthand of vector operators)

$$\nabla \cdot (k \nabla T) = \rho c_v \partial T/\partial t - S \tag{6.1}$$

where t is time, ρ is density, c_v specific heat capacity and S a heat source.

We shall show in the next chapter exactly how this equation can be derived from first principles of energy conservation. For the moment let us take the equation for granted and look at the things that appear in it.

∇ stands for the space-derivative operator which in Cartesian (x, y, z) coordinates is

$$\mathbf{i} \frac{\partial}{\partial x} + \mathbf{j} \frac{\partial}{\partial y} + \mathbf{k} \frac{\partial}{\partial z}$$

where **i**, **j** and **k** are unit vectors in the x, y and z directions respectively. The derivative $\partial/\partial x$ is a 'partial derivative' and just means 'pretend that y and z are constants and differentiate with respect to x as if it were the only independent variable'. The same goes for $\partial/\partial y$ and $\partial/\partial z$. The dot in equation (6.1) means 'take the dot product (the scalar product)'. But we shall not be using vectors any more, so it does not matter if you have never used the shorthand of vector operators.

The left-hand side of equation (6.1) written out in full for cartesian co-ordinates in two dimensions is then

$$\frac{\partial}{\partial x}\left(k\,\frac{\partial T}{\partial x}\right) + \frac{\partial}{\partial y}\left(k\,\frac{\partial T}{\partial y}\right)$$

You will often see this simplified to

$$k\left(\frac{\partial^2 T}{\partial x^2} + \frac{\partial^2 T}{\partial y^2}\right)$$

but this form is true only if k is constant in space — that is, if it does not change its value from point to point. The essence of the method we shall develop for solving equation (6.1) is to allow for varying values of k, so we shall use the slightly more complicated form for the left-hand side of the equation.

The physical quantities $(x, y, z, k, t, \ldots)$ need hold no fears for us. When I was at school we worked in a crazy set of 'units' which involved feet, pounds, centimetres and curious things called British Thermal Units. In fact, until the 1950s, we were still expected to know about rods, poles and/or perches, bushels and pecks, ... Nowadays all that is gone and we can work in SI (International System, French 'Système International') units which mean that we need not even think about units provided we stick to metres for all the lengths, kilogrammes for masses, degrees Celsius (Centigrade) or Kelvin — either will do (K's are just °C's plus 273) — for temperature, Joules for energy and seconds for time. The beauty of SI units is that if you feed in data in SI your output is always in SI. The cleverest thing of all is that the SI unit for mechanical power (1 Watt which is 1 Joule per second) is identical to the unit of electrical power (1 Watt, which is 1 Volt × 1 Ampere) — so it does not matter whether we work with electrical energy or mechanical energy, and we can mix the two without worrying. Remember, though, metres not centimetres and kilogrammes not grammes.

The thermal conductivity k is a measure of the ease with which thermal energy can be conducted through a substance: for copper, k is 393 Watts per metre per (degree) Kelvin (or per degree Celsius) and for air it is 0.0262 W/m/K, so it makes quite a difference what substance you are dealing with!

The density ρ is an old schoolfriend: as you see from equation (6.1) (or from common sense if you prefer) the denser a substance the more thermal energy required to change its temperature by 1 degree. The units are kilogrammes per cubic metre and a cubic metre is pretty gigantic — 1 cubic metre of water weighs one tonne — but we are stuck with it if we are using SI units. So the density of copper is 8960 kg per cubic metre and that of water is 1000 (not 1!).

More Ambitious Applications: the Heat Equation

The specific heat capacity c_v is the heat required to raise one unit mass of a substance through one degree of temperature. It is obvious that this will vary from substance to substance: it takes a lot more work to heat up a kilogramme of water (c_v = 4180 Joule/Kelvin/kg) than to heat up the same mass of aluminium (900 Joule/Kelvin/kg) or copper (385 J/kg/K).

All the values given are for room temperature (about 25°C or 298 K).

As you may realise, the 'source term' on the right-hand side of equation (6.1) must be a quantity measured in the same units as the rest of the equation: the rest of the right-hand side is in terms of kg/m/m/m ∗ J/kg/K ∗ K/s — that is, Watts per cubic metre. It is a measure of the input of thermal power per unit volume (or units of energy input per second per unit volume, which is the same thing in SI units).

As special cases, equation (6.1) includes

(i) Laplace's equation: $\nabla^2 \phi = 0$
   We get this by having no time variation ($\partial T/\partial t = 0$), no source term ($S = 0$), and renaming T as ϕ.
(ii) Poisson's equation $\nabla^2 \phi = -S$
   This time we have a source term, but the rest is as for Laplace's equation.
(iii) The Navier–Stokes equation for fluid flow, for the special case of a fluid moving steadily in one direction

$$\nabla \cdot (\mu \nabla U) = dp/dz$$

S has become the pressure-gradient ($-dp/dz$), T is the velocity U and k is the viscosity μ. Again the time-dependence is suppressed ($\partial T/\partial t = 0$). As we are using SI units, we just set the pressure-gradient in Newtons/square metre/metre, the viscosity in Newton-seconds/square metre and out comes the velocity in metres per second.

These are just a few examples of how the solution of equation (6.1) leads us to the solution of an enormous class of equations that arise in electromagnetism, in fluid mechanics and aerodynamics, and in every branch of potential theory, quite apart from time-dependent heat transfer. Other applications include stresses in solids, and the stretching of membranes. As we said in chapter 1, the ability to solve second-order partial differential equations like equation (6.1) covers a vast part of the theory that engineers, physicists and mathematicians have to deal with. And equation (6.1) is a quite general one, with a very wide range of applications.

The particular form of the heat equation that we have chosen in equation (6.1) assumes, without the loss of too much generality, that k may vary in space but not in time, and that ρ and c_v are constant in both space and time. In fact the solution procedure that we shall use for equation (6.1) will allow us, if we like, to relax these conditions.

In due course, in order to derive an accurate finite-difference model of equation (6.1), we shall derive it from first principles, so do not worry if it is not yet obvious to you why it should be the equation that governs the conduction of heat. All will become clear. For the moment, let us just treat (6.1) as an equation worth solving.

6.2 A Simple Form of the Equation

If k is constant, equation (6.1) may be written as

$$\nabla^2 T = (1/a)(\partial T/\partial t) - S/k \tag{6.2}$$

and in the 'steady state' — when there is no time variation (or no further time variation) — equation (6.2) becomes

$$\nabla^2 T = -S/k$$

If there is only one space dimension of any importance, equation (6.1) tends to

$$\partial^2 T/\partial x^2 = (1/a)\, \partial T/\partial t - S/k \tag{6.3}$$

where, of course, we have to use partial derivatives because although there is only one space dimension involved we have a second independent variable — time.

If time is not important — that is, if the problem has settled into a 'steady state' — writing $-S/k$ as $f(x)$

$$d^2 T/dx^2 = f(x) \qquad\qquad \text{our old friend (2.5)}$$

Now, $a = k/(\rho\, c_v)$ is known as the *thermal diffusivity*. From its dimensions (area per unit time) which involve the reciprocal of time it is clearly a measure of the rate at which temperature changes diffuse through the body.

6.3 The Finite-difference Form

Equation (6.3) can very easily be written in finite-difference form. The left-hand side represents the variation of T in space with time held constant, while the right-hand side represents the variation of T in time at a fixed point in space. The source, S/k, can be on either side since it is assumed to be constant in space and time.

Figure 6.1 shows the $T(x, t)$ surface.

We can use equation (2.7) to put the left-hand side of equation (6.3) into finite-difference form, with the dependent variable now called not y but T and with constant space-interval Dx

$$\text{left-hand side} = (T(I+1, t) - 2*T(I, t) + T(I-1, t))/(Dx * Dx)$$

For the right-hand side we write

$$\ldots = (T(I, t+Dt) - T(I, t))/(Dt) - S/k \tag{6.4}$$

More Ambitious Applications: the Heat Equation

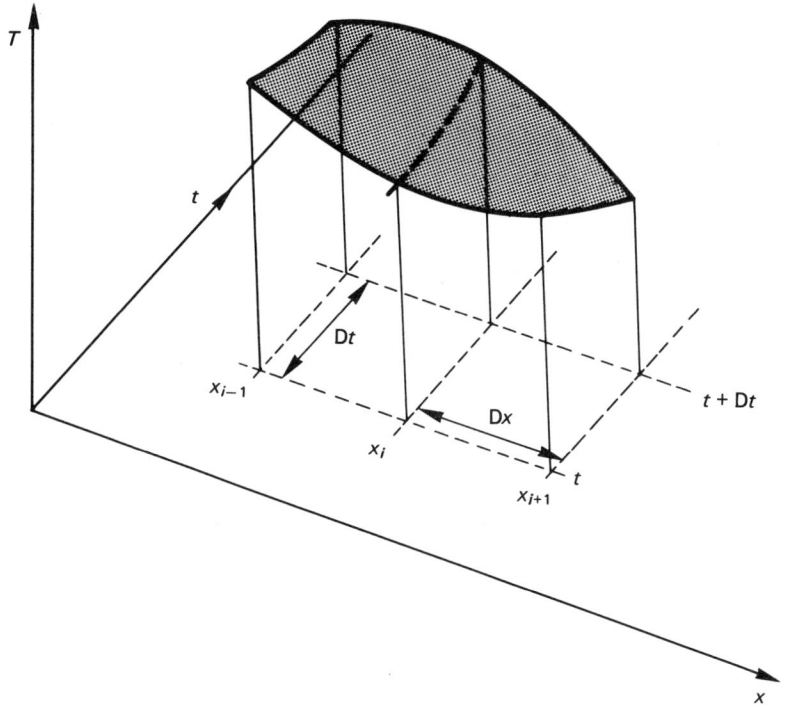

Figure 6.1

But we now have to decide whether to evaluate the left-hand side at time t or at time $t + Dt$ — or perhaps at some time between the two. For reasons which will emerge later, we say that if we evaluate the left-hand side at time t, we get an 'explicit' formula, while if we evaluate the left-hand side at time $t + Dt$ we get an 'implicit' formula for $T(I, t + Dt)$.

For clarity let us write $T(I, t + Dt)$ as $T(I)^+$ and $T(I, t)$ as $T(I)^-$.

The problem is simply to find the values of $T(I, t + Dt)$ in terms of the values of $T(I, t + Dt)$ and $T(I, t)$. By writing the left-hand side of (6.4) in terms of $T(I, t)$ we can get an expression for $T(I, t + Dt)$, which we do not know, in terms that involve only the values of $T(I, t)$, which we do know.

The explicit version of expression (6.4) is (reversing the left-hand side and right-hand side to make things clearer from here on)

$$\frac{T_i^+ - T_i^-}{aDt} = \frac{T_{i+1}^- - 2T_i^- + T_{i-1}^-}{Dx * Dx} + \frac{S}{k} \tag{6.5}$$

If we write aDt/Dx^2 as R (the 'Fourier number' for our cell), we have

$$T_i^+ = \frac{Sa\,Dt}{k} + T_i^- + R(T_{i+1}^- - 2T_i^- + T_{i-1}^-)$$

or

$$T_i^+ = \frac{Sa\,Dt}{k} + RT_{i+1}^- + (1 - 2R)T_i^- + RT_{i-1}^- \tag{6.6}$$

Equation (6.6) is an explicit expression for the unknown T in terms of the known quantities T. Hence the designation 'explicit'.

Equation (6.6) is, alas, too good to be true for all Dt. For equation (6.6) not to be patent nonsense, R must be less than or equal to 0.5. Otherwise, the coefficient of $T(i, t)$ is negative: this means that the lower the temperature at the point i at time t, the higher it will be at the same point an instant later. This would be ridiculous and just goes to show that we can use the old temperatures to forecast the new ones for just so far into the future and no further. The limit is $R = 0.5$. This in turn means that to get to steady state — when there are no noticeable further changes in temperature, which happens at about $R = 10$ in many physical situations — we should have to take a large number of little timesteps.

Equation (6.6) has the sole advantage that its solution does not require iteration. However, as we have already seen, there is no reason why the implicit counterpart of equation (6.6)

$$T_i^+ = \frac{Sa\,Dt}{k} + T_i^- + R(T_{i+1}^+ - 2T_i^+ + T_{i-1}^+)$$

or

$$(1 + 2R)T_i^+ = \frac{Sa\,Dt}{k} + T_i^- + R(T_{i+1}^+ + T_{i-1}^+) \tag{6.7}$$

should not be rearranged to succumb to the TDMA. In fact, equation (6.7) is just equation (2.10) again

```
Y(I) = (G1*Y(I+1) + G2*Y(I-1) + G3)/G4                    (2.10)
```

with

$G1 = 1$
$G2 = 1$
$G4 = 2 + (1/R)$ \hfill (6.8)

and

$$G3 = (1/R)T_i^- + \frac{S\,Dx\,.\,Dx}{k}$$

More Ambitious Applications: the Heat Equation

So we can actually use Program 7 or its later modifications to solve the heat equation (6.1) in one space and one time dimension.

The explicit formula could not work for large values of R. The implicit formula on the other hand will converge to the solution for any value of R however large.

If we look at equation (6.7) we can see that the sum of the coefficients of the unknowns on the right-hand side after dividing through by $(1 + 2R)$ to get an equation for $T(i, t + Dt)$ is less than 1, since $R/(1 + 2R)$ is less than 0.5 for all values of R. This means that the implicit formula satisfies the 'diagonal dominance' criterion that we mentioned at the end of chapter 3 and that it will therefore converge for all R.

Program 11
(Suitable as listed for the IBM PC or the Apple II)

The modifications for Program 7 for this problem are as follows

```
2010  REM FNF(X) NOT NEEDED
2020  INPUT "ENTER CELL FOURIER NO :";R
2030  INPUT "ENTER CONDUCTIVITY :";K
2040  INPUT "ENTER HEAT SOURCE :";S
2110  G1 = 1
2120  G2 = 1
2130  G4 = 2 + 1 / R

4002  GOSUB 5000
4022  G3 = Y(I) / R + S * DX * DX / K
4120  REM
4130  REM
4200  REM   ALWAYS CONVERGES
4210  GOSUB 9800
4220  GOTO 4015

5002  PRINT "TEMPERATURES AT FO = ";C3 * DX * DX / L / L * R
```

We force the program to move on to the next time step without iterating. In fact, if lines 4200–4220 are left unchanged in Program 7 the program will appear to iterate. Line 4022 is reached during each iteration, so that the value of G3 would be updated as a new value of Y(I) is obtained. This is wrong, as the value needed for Y(I) in 4022 is the *old* value — the one at time t, and not the one at $t + Dt$, which is what Y(I) will iterate to. So we must now take courage and cut out the luxury of a second 'checking' iteration at each time step. Line 4210 uses the array plotter at 9800 rather than the whole graphics module: this has the effect of superimposing the graphs on the same axes without erasing the screen.

Now we can start solving real problems, just as we said at the beginning of this chapter.

Exercises 6.1

Exercise 6.1.1. Use Program 11 suitably modified to solve the problem of a steel bar 1 metre long, insulated all round (except at the ends), initially at room temperature — say 20° Celsius — and suddenly heated at one end to 100° Celsius while the other end remains fixed at 20° Celsius.

Exercise 6.1.2. Use Program 11 further modified, using the update for gradient boundary conditions, to solve the problem of the metre-long bar when it is heated at one end as in exercise 6.1.1 but this time insulated at the other end. Use Program 12.

Program 12
(Suitable as listed for the IBM PC or the Apple II)

As Program 11 except as follows

```
3010  INPUT "ENTER GRADIENT AT X(1) ";G

4002  GOSUB 5000

4048  D(2) = D(2) + A(2)
4050  B(2) = B(2) + A(2) * G * DX

4200  Y(1) = Y(2) - G * DX
```

You should get output which looks like figure 6.2.

The curves are for steps of $R = 0.05$. If you adjust the value of cell-Fourier-number suitably, for 19 nodes, you should get the output shown.

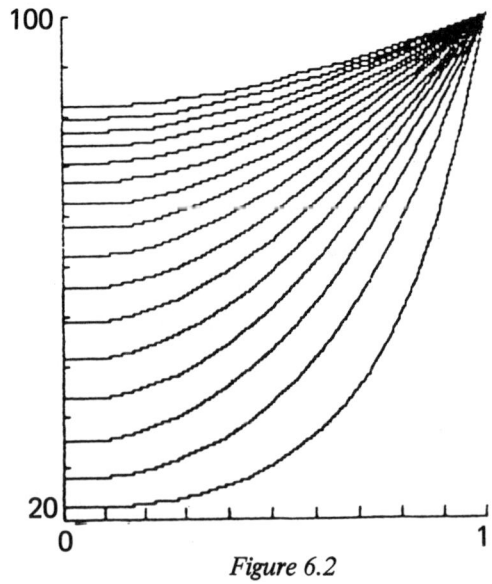

Figure 6.2

7 Two-dimensional Phenomena — a Glimpse of Reality

7.1 Heat Conduction in Two Dimensions

The real world is, happily, neither one-dimensional nor yet specially three-dimensional in general. This is good news, as one-dimensional models of reality tend to be trivial and the three-dimensional ones are mostly too large to fit on present-day computers. A quick calculation shows that a typical problem such as the ones we have looked at in chapter 4 requiring 99 nodes in one dimension will require 99 * 99 * 99 nodes in three dimensions. If one needs to store, say, ten items of information about each node, this will mean something like 10 000 000 items in all. It is easy to see that a reasonably complicated three-dimensional problem might require more capacity than is readily available on all but the very largest computers. The problems may also take an enormous length of time to iterate to convergence.

The equation is still

$$\nabla \cdot (k \nabla T) = \rho c_v \, \partial T / \partial t - S \tag{6.1}$$

which in two-dimensional Cartesian coordinates gives

$$\frac{\partial}{\partial x} \left(k \frac{\partial T}{\partial x} \right) + \frac{\partial}{\partial y} \left(k \frac{\partial T}{\partial y} \right) = \rho c_v \frac{\partial T}{\partial t} - S \tag{7.1}$$

and in two-dimensional cylindrical polar coordinates (r and z, the problem being assumed axi-symmetric — no variation with respect to θ) this becomes

$$\frac{\partial}{\partial z} \left(k \frac{\partial T}{\partial z} \right) + \frac{1}{r} \frac{\partial}{\partial r} \left(kr \frac{\partial T}{\partial r} \right) = \rho c_v \frac{\partial T}{\partial t} - S$$

If we mark with an '*' the r's in equation (7.2) that are not part of differential operators

$$\frac{\partial}{\partial z} \left(k \frac{\partial T}{\partial z} \right) + \frac{1}{r^*} \frac{\partial}{\partial r} \left(kr^* \frac{\partial T}{\partial r} \right) = \rho c_v \frac{\partial T}{\partial t} - S \tag{7.2}$$

we can see that the only difference between equations (7.1) and (7.2) is that (7.2) has r^*'s and (7.1) does not. If we simply put $r^* = 1$ in (7.2) we get (7.1). So (7.1) is just a special case of (7.2) obtained by taking the limit such that r is not very different from one end of the solution domain to the other. This is, for example, true on the surface of a very large sphere. That is why the earth is flat (at least for all usual practical purposes: we do not bother to consider the difference in gravity between our heads and our toes).

Figure 7.1 shows the solution domains for Cartesian and cylindrical polar coordinates. We assume that there is no variation in either case in the direction normal to the paper. We also assume that we are working with a unit thickness in that direction. In the case of cylindrical polars this means a unit angle of rotation in the θ sense (that is, 1 radian). This convention is just to simplify the calculations — since there is no variation in the direction normal to the paper it does not actually matter how deep the solid is assumed to be, but if it is one unit deep then the volumes of the cells are equal to their cross-sectional areas times r^*.

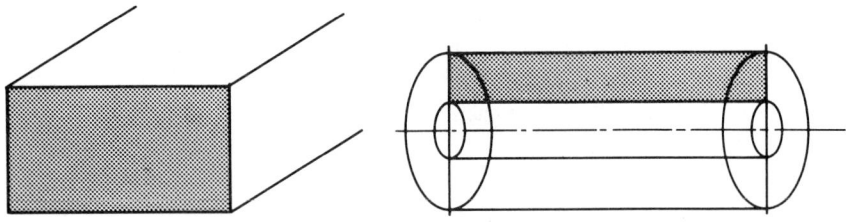

Figure 7.1

7.2 Deriving the Heat Equation

Figure 7.2 shows a 'control volume'. This is just an arbitrary little box that we draw in our solid so that we can consider very carefully what goes on inside and what crosses the boundaries. What we are trying to do is just like calculating the annual change in the population of the island of Britain: this must be equal to the number of people born in Britain during the year minus the number who died plus the number that came in from abroad minus the ones who emigrated. In this case we are trying to balance the heat account for the control volume. Heat is conserved so that the (net) heat flowing into the control volume across the faces plus the internal generation of heat must be equal to the change in internal energy inside the control volume.

The control volume in figure 7.2 is just one 'cell': a node surrounded by grid lines. We can see not only the node, P, but also the nodes E east of P, W west of P, N north of P and S south of P. The grid lines are drawn to bisect the distances between P and its neighbours.

Two-dimensional Phenomena – a Glimpse of Reality

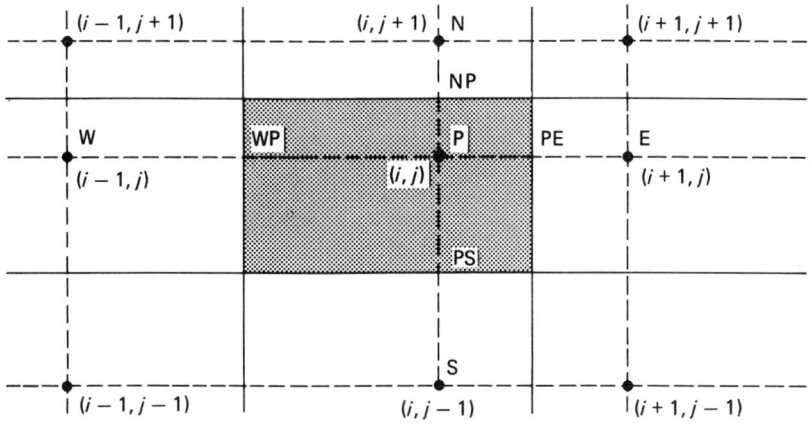

Figure 7.2

Let us calculate the individual components of the heat balance. We shall make things a little easier by assuming that we can work with a Cartesian rather than polar system.

First of all the heat generated within the control volume, which we shall assume to be one unit deep (in the direction normal to the paper): this is given by S, the rate of generation per unit volume and per unit time. So in one unit of time, the amount of heat generated in the control volume is

$S\, \mathrm{D}x\, \mathrm{D}y$

Next, the rate of increase of internal energy: this is

$$\frac{\partial E}{\partial t} \rho\, \mathrm{D}x\, \mathrm{D}y = c_\mathrm{v} \frac{\partial T}{\partial t} \rho\, \mathrm{D}x\, \mathrm{D}y$$

For the third component of the heat balance, we must use Fourier's Law, which says that the amount of heat conducted in, say, the x-direction, across the cell in one unit of time is

$$-\frac{\partial}{\partial x}\left(-k\frac{\partial T}{\partial x}\mathrm{D}y\right)\mathrm{D}x$$

where the $\mathrm{D}y$ (times 1, for the unit depth of the cell) represents the cross-sectional area of the faces at WP and PE in figure 7.2. Similarly for the y-direction, we get (going from bottom to top – that is, for increasing values of y)

$$-\frac{\partial}{\partial y}\left(-k\frac{\partial T}{\partial y}\mathrm{D}x\right)\mathrm{D}y$$

Microcomputer Modelling by Finite Differences

If we combine these components to form the heat balance for the cell, we get

Heat flow in + Heat generated within = Net heat increase

that is

$$-\frac{\partial}{\partial x}\left(-k\frac{\partial T}{\partial x}Dy\right)Dx - \frac{\partial}{\partial y}\left(-k\frac{\partial T}{\partial y}Dx\right)Dy + S\,Dx\,Dy = \rho\,c_v\frac{\partial T}{\partial t}Dx\,Dy$$

which is effectively the same as equation (7.1).

7.3 The Finite-difference Form of the Equation

From equation (7.2), which we shall use because it is the more general form of the heat equation, the precise form of the finite-difference model of the net heat conduction across the control volume from left to right will be

$$\frac{k_{PE}\dfrac{T_E^+ - T_P^+}{z_E - z_P} - k_{WP}\dfrac{T_P^+ - T_W^+}{z_P - z_W}}{z_{PE} - z_{WP}} \quad \text{at time } (t + Dt) \tag{7.3}$$

Similarly, the expression for the net heat flow rate from bottom to top of the control volume will be

$$\frac{1}{r_P^*}\frac{k_{PN}r_{PN}^*\dfrac{T_N^+ - T_P^+}{r_N - r_P} - k_{SP}r_{SP}^*\dfrac{T_P^+ - T_S^+}{r_P - r_S}}{r_{PN} - r_{SP}} \quad \text{at time } (t + Dt) \tag{7.4}$$

So the sum of expressions (7.3) and (7.4) will be equal to

$$\rho\,c_v\frac{T_P^+ - T_P^-}{Dt} - S$$

7.4 The Model of k_{PN} etc.

As you can see from expressions (7.3) and (7.4) we need a model for the values of k at PN, SP, WP and PE. This is important as k must be allowed to vary from node to node. It might seem reasonable to use a linear interpolation for k

$$k_{PN} = (k_P + k_N)/2 \tag{7.5}$$

However, there is a good reason for treating k as an exception to our general rule of using linear interpolation wherever possible. Equation (7.5) gives rise to a paradox.

Consider a discontinuity in material: this will happen whenever a solid is composed of two different substances. We shall arrange the grid so as to have the discontinuity coincide with the boundary of a control volume — for example, at the point WP — so that equation (7.5) would mean that the value of k at WP was the average of the two conductivities on either side of WP. Now, if we have a (near-)perfect insulator on one side (k is nearly zero at W and throughout the cell surrounding W), equation (7.5) tells us that the effective conductivity from W to P will be $k/2$. This will mean that there will be a non-zero amount of heat conducted through the adiabatic wall at WP. This is nonsense: if there is zero conductivity between W and P no heat can pass between W and P. So we must find a better model for the value of k at WP.

We turn to Ohm's Law for the solution to our problem, because the same problem arises in problems of electrical conduction. We know that we can add two resistances in series (figure 7.3).

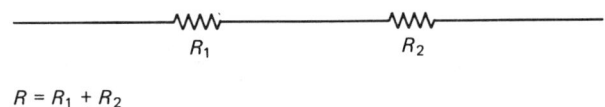

$R = R_1 + R_2$

Figure 7.3

The analogy for heat — where we use thermal resistances rather than electrical ones, but the principle remains the same — is shown in figure 7.4.

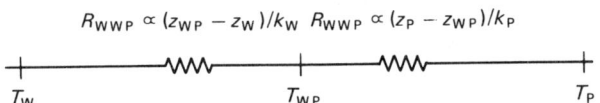

Figure 7.4

$$\frac{1}{k_{WP}}(z_P - z_W) = \frac{1}{k_W}(z_{WP} - z_W) + \frac{1}{k_P}(z_W - z_{WP})$$

Now, WP is defined as the mid-point of the line joining W and P, so that

$$k_{WP} = \frac{2 k_W k_P}{k_W + k_P} \qquad (7.6)$$

and we shall use (7.6) rather than (7.5) for our value of k at WP.

Let us check: if the values of k at W and P are the same, we want the value of k at WP to be the same too. Equation (7.6) confirms this.

If k tends to zero at either W or P, so does the value of k at WP as given by (7.6), so that our paradox has disappeared: we shall have zero conduction through an adiabatic wall, as is only right and proper.

If k at W (say) tends to infinity, k at WP will tend to twice the value of k at P. This, as we shall see shortly, ensures that the temperatures at W and WP are the same (and correct): in other words, there is no temperature variation within a perfect conductor.

7.5 Boundary Conditions

If in figure 7.4 the point WP lies on a physical boundary, with W outside the body and P inside it, we have to have boundary conditions relating the temperature at W (outside) to the temperature at P (inside). These may take several forms. Because our formula (7.6) allows us to provide for sudden discontinuities of material, we shall be able to use it to specify our boundary conditions via the thermal conductivities. If we know the temperatures at W and at P, we shall be able to calculate the temperature at WP (the actual boundary) by using the formula

$$\frac{T_W - T_{WP}}{T_{WP} - T_W} = \frac{1/k_W}{1/k_P}$$

that is

$$T_{WP} = (k_W T_W + k_P T_P)/(k_W + k_P) \qquad (7.7)$$

which should be familiar from elementary electric circuit theory, with temperature drop replacing voltage drop.

Adiabatic boundary

This is the easiest to specify. If the boundary is adiabatic, we merely have to set the value of k at W to a vanishingly small number: then k at WP will also be effectively zero. Formula (7.7) tells us that

$$T_{WP} = T_P$$

which tells us that $\partial T/\partial z = 0$ at an adiabatic boundary, which it should be.

Fixed-temperature boundaries

To fix the temperature at the boundary WP to some definite value, we

(a) set T_W to the boundary value
(b) set k_W to an enormous number.

Then, as we have already seen, formula (7.6) gives us

$$k_{WP} = 2 k_P$$

Two-dimensional Phenomena – a Glimpse of Reality

and formula (7.7) gives

$$T_{WP} = T_W$$

as it should be.

A none-too-serious warning: though the method we have adopted for setting boundary values is very effective and nearly foolproof, the fact is that a very small number (say 1E−10) is not actually equal to zero, so that given long enough a bit of heat will leak out through an 'adiabatic' boundary specified in this way. It is important to choose your 'zero' and your 'infinitely large number' to suit your computer, and occasionally to suit your problem. The fact that we do not actually use zero or infinity corresponds, if you like, to the fact that there are no perfect conductors in nature nor truly fixed-temperature boundary conditions – nor yet perfectly adiabatic walls either.

Finite heat transfer at the boundaries

The whole point of treating transient (time-varying) heat transfer as opposed to considering only steady-state problems is to study the behaviour of a body as time passes. We shall consider what happens if a finite amount of heat is allowed to escape per unit time and per unit area across the various surfaces of the body.

One common specification of such a boundary condition is to stipulate that

$k*$ (temperature-gradient across the boundary)
$= h*$ (temperature-difference between the boundary and the outside)

where h is a surface heat transfer coefficient. We then have a boundary set-up as shown in figure 7.5.

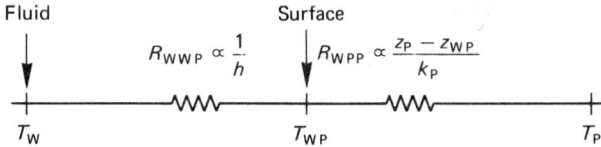

Figure 7.5

Comparing figure 7.5 with figure 7.4 we can see that we must replace the quantity

$$(z_{WP} - z_W)/k_W$$

by the quantity

$$1/h$$

and we thus must replace k_W by $h(z_{WP} - z_W)$.

This means that we shall specify our boundary condition by means of a 'notional conductivity'

$$k_W = h(z_P - z_W)/2 \qquad (7.8)$$

If we take (7.8) as the general form of the boundary condition, we need simply to set the appropriate value of h (rather than k) to

(i) a very large number for fixed temperatures
(ii) a very small number for adiabatic boundaries
(iii) an ordinary-sized number for a finite surface heat-transfer coefficient.

It is much more natural to specify boundaries in this way than if we were to have to set an effective conductivity, as the usual way of distinguishing different boundary conditions in problems of the kind that we shall tackle is by means of either the surface heat-transfer coefficient or via the 'Biot number'. This is the number

$$hL/k$$

where L is some characteristic length of the body (measured in the direction in which the heat is being transferred): we can see from equation (7.8) that the Biot number is non-dimensional.

A very large Biot number is equivalent to a fixed-temperature boundary condition and a very small one corresponds to an adiabatic boundary. The strictly correct way of specifying the boundary condition is by means of the Biot number, because this insures against, for example, the consequences of having a very large value of L or a very small one of k, which would mean that we should have to use an even smaller value of h than otherwise would be the case for effectively zero heat transfer across the boundary. However, if we stick to numbers like 1E−10 or smaller, we are unlikely to run up against such difficulties even if we use the surface heat-transfer coefficient to specify the boundary condition − as we shall.

Gradient-type boundary conditions

Another common type of boundary condition is where we are told how much heat can escape through a boundary per unit area and per unit time: this is a 'specified heat flux' condition. We can use Fourier's Law to derive an expression for the value of the ('free-stream') temperature outside the body at W, for a given value Q of the heat flux. As we are concerned only with the gradient of T we may consider the body effectively extended to include the point W − that is, k at WP is to be taken as the same as k at P.

We have

$$\begin{aligned} Q &= -k\, \partial T/\partial z \\ &= -k\,(T_P - T_W)/(z_P - z_W) \end{aligned}$$

Two-dimensional Phenomena – a Glimpse of Reality

$Q(z_P - z_W)/k = T_W - T_P$

$T_W = T_P + Q(z_P - z_W)/k$

$T_{WP} = T_P + Q(z_P - z_W)/(2k)$

Clearly, in the light of our earlier experience (chapter 4) of setting gradient-type boundary conditions, we shall have to incorporate the information about the specified heat-flux into the coefficients rather than risk unnecessary iteration.

8 The THC (Transient Heat Conduction) Computer Program

8.1 Introduction

In chapters 1-7 we collected together all the components necessary for constructing a general-purpose computer program for solving two-dimensional problems in heat transfer, electromagnetic theory and fluid dynamics. In fact, the only new idea we need to grapple with is that our dependent variable has acquired an extra subscript. We shall take advantage of the greater flexibility introduced by the way we calculate the grid-spacing (chapter 5) and the conductivity (chapter 7). Otherwise the equations are essentially the same as the ones we met in chapter 2. Above all, the equations remain more or less tri-diagonal.

The structure of the THC program is exactly as before (Suitable for IBM PC or for the Apple II as listed)

```
1 REM MAIN PROGRAM SECTION: LINES 1-999
999 STOP

1000 REM SUBROUTINE START FOR INITIALISATION
1999 RETURN

2000 REM SUBROUTINE PHYS FOR THE PHYSICAL PROPERTIES
2999 RETURN

3000 REM SUBROUTINE EDGE FOR SETTING BOUNDARY CONDITIONS
3999 RETURN

4000 REM SUBROUTINE WORK FOR CALCULATING THE SOLUTION
4999 RETURN

5000 REM SUBROUTINE PLOT FOR PRINTING AND PLOTTING RESULTS
5999 RETURN

9000 REM SUBROUTINE DRAW: GRAPHICS AT 9100 ETC.
9999 RETURN
```

8.2 The MAIN Control Segment (1-999)

The MAIN segment of the THC program is illustrated in the stylised flowchart of figure 8.1.

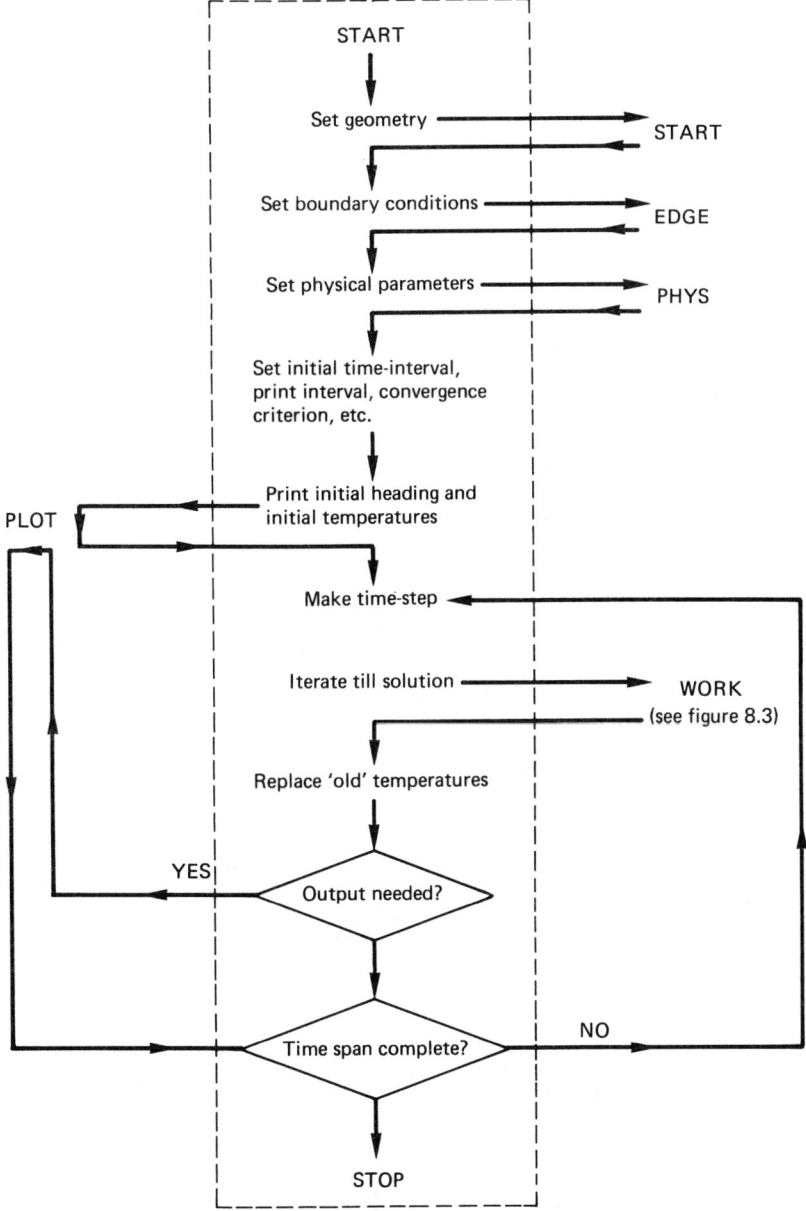

Figure 8.1

After calls to the subroutines at 1000 (START), 3000 (EDGE), 2000 (PHYS), T1 (starting time in seconds — normally set to zero), T2 (time-increment) and factor T8 for increasing the subsequent time-increments are set. The order of the routines at 2000 and 3000 is dictated not by the fact that we call them in a particular sequence at the outset but because we shall not normally expect to revisit the routines at 1000 and 2000 at later times, while that at 3000 (EDGE) will be required subsequently if we have time-dependent boundary conditions.

The value of the convergence criterion C2 is set at line 170. We shall see that the value we have chosen is suitable when we come to try out particular problems. The variable N7 determines how frequently the convergence of the iterative procedure is monitored. For time-dependent problems this is best left set at 1. If T2 is chosen to be very large, so as to give steady-state solutions (a Fourier number of 20 is quite sufficient to ensure this), N7 is automatically reset to 30. Likewise the variable E1 is used as a time (in seconds) beyond which the time-steps should not be allowed to proceed. The setting of 10 000 may not be satisfactory for some purposes — in fact, of course, E1 should be calculated to give a Fourier number of (say) 100 rather than being set in seconds.

We have to provide explicitly for the time-step, which occurs between lines 260 and 410. The newly calculated temperatures have to be stored as 'old' temperatures, so that they can be used in calculating the next lot of new temperatures.

When the program has determined that the time-stepping procedure is over, a test is made for whether the current information has been printed out. If not, the PLOT routine is called (GOSUB 5000).

We shall work throughout in SI units — normally in metres, kilograms, seconds etc.

The cast of variables, in order of appearance in MAIN (though not all necessarily used there), is

Variable	Line	Purpose
A(12), B(12), C(12), D(12)	25	coefficients for TDMA
K(12,12)	30	thermal conductivity
N(12,12), O(12,12)	30	new (N) and old (O) temperatures
P(12,12)	30	used in PLOT
Q(12,12)	30	heat source
R(12)	35	r-coordinates (y-coordinates)
S(12,12)	35	effective conductivities at SP
W(12,12)	35	effective conductivities at WP
Z(12)	35	z-coordinates (y-coordinates)
T1	140	elapsed time in seconds
T2	151	initial time-step Dt

The THC (Transient Heat Conduction) Computer Program 71

T8	153	time-step enlargement factor
C2	170	convergence criterion
N7	190	iterations between monitoring
E1	220	maximum time in seconds
P1	360	print-interval in seconds (set in PLOT)

The MAIN control segment of the program is

```
0    REM APPLE REQUIRES "LOMEM:24576"
1    PRINT CHR$(12) : REM CLEAR SCREEN - APPLE USES "HOME"
10   PRINT "IBM PC VERSION OF THE THC PROGRAM"
20   REM  DIMENSION ALL ARRAYS NEEDED
25      DIM A(12), B(12), C(12), D(12)
30      DIM K(12,12), N(12,12), O(12,12), P(12,12), Q(12,12)
35      DIM R(12), S(12,12), W(12,12), Z(12)
40   REM  MAIN PROGRAM CONTROL SEGMENT
50   REM  CALL START TO SET GEOMETRY AND GRID
60      GOSUB 1000
70   REM  CALL EDGE TO SET BOUNDARY CONDITIONS
80      GOSUB 3000
90   REM  CALL PHYS TO SET PHYSICAL PARAMETERS
100     GOSUB 2000
110  REM  SET INITIAL TIME- AND PRINT- INTERVALS
140     T1 = 0
150     PRINT "ENTER INITIAL TIME STEP ";
151     INPUT T2
152     PRINT "ENTER FACTOR BY WHICH TIME-STEP
              IS TO BE ALTERED AT EACH STEP ";
153     INPUT T8
160  REM  C2 IS CONVERGENCE CRITERION
170     C2 = .0002 * (I1 - 2) * (J1 - 2)
180  REM  SET ITERATION PRINT CHECK N7
190     N7 = 1
200     IF T2 > = L9 / 10000 THEN N7 = 30
210  REM  STOP TIME E1
220     E1 = 10000
230  REM  PRINT INITIAL DISTRIBUTION
240    GOSUB 5000
250  REM  MAKE TIME STEP
260        T1 = T1 + T2
270        REM  ITERATE TILL SOLUTION FOR TIME T1
280        GOSUB 4000
290        REM  UPDATE TEMPERATURES
300        FOR J = 1 TO J1: FOR I = 1 TO I1
320            O(I,J) = N(I,J)
330        NEXT I: NEXT J
350        REM  TEST WHETHER OUTPUT NEEDED
360        IF T1 > = P1 THEN GOSUB 5000
370        REM  TEST FOR STOP CONDITION
380        IF T1 > E1 THEN 430
390        REM INCREASE TIME STEP LENGTH
```

```
405         T2 = T2 * T8
410         GOTO 260
420 REM  TIME STEP ENDS HERE
430  IF T1< = P1 THEN GOSUB 5000
999  STOP
```

8.3 The START Subroutine (1000-1999)

The variables introduced in START are

S9	1030	small number ("zero") 1e-10
L9	1040	large number ("infinity") 1e10
P3	1060	PI (3.14159..)
P4	1080	switch for Cartesian (0) / axisymmetric (1)
I1	1120	no. of nodes in I direction
J1	1160	no. of nodes in J direction
R1	1180-1210	internal radius for cylindrical coordinates
H1	1250	height of calculation zone
W1	1290	width of calculation zone
F1	1320	grid-expansion factor for z (or x) direction
F2	1340	grid-expansion factor for r (or y) direction
D1	1350	Z(2)-Z(1
D2	1360	R(2)-R(1)
O(1,1)	1520	initial temperature inside solid

The START subroutine of the THC program (1000-1999) is

```
1000 REM   SUBROUTINE START  FOR GRID AND GEOMETRY
1010 REM   THERE ARE I1 NODES IN Z DIRN., J1 IN Y (OR R) DIRN
1020 REM   S9 IS A SMALL £, L9 A LARGE ONE
1030     S9 = 1E - 10
1040     L9 = 1E10
1050 REM   P3 IS PI, I.E. 3.14159...
1060     P3 = ATN (1) * 4
1070 REM P4=0: PLANE GEOMETRY/ P4=1:SYMMETRY ABOUT Y=0 AXIS
1080     INPUT "PLANE GEOMETRY (0) OR AXISYMMETRIC (1) ";P4
1090     A$(0) = "X"
1100     A$(1) = "Z"
1110     PRINT "NO.OF NODES IN ";A$(P4);" DIR'N = ";
1120     INPUT I1
1130     B$(0) = "Y"
1140     B$(1) = "R"
1150     PRINT "NO.OF NODES IN ";B$(P4);" DIR'N = ";
1160     INPUT J1
1170 REM   H1 IS THICKNESS AND W1 IS WIDTH IN METRES
1180     R1 = 0
1190     IF P4 = 0 THEN 1220
1200     PRINT "INTERNAL RADIUS (METRES) (0 FOR SOLID CYLINDER) = ";
1210     INPUT R1
```

The THC (Transient Heat Conduction) Computer Program 73

```
1220    C$(0) = "HEIGHT"
1230    C$(1) = "RADIAL THICKNESS"
1240     PRINT C$(P4);" (IN METRES) = ";
1250     INPUT H1
1260    D$(0) = "WIDTH"
1270    D$(1) = "LENGTH OF CYLINDER"
1280     PRINT D$(P4);" (IN METRES) = ";
1290     INPUT W1
1300  REM F1, F2 EXPANSION FACTORS FOR GRID IN Z, Y (OR R) DIRNS
1310     PRINT "GRID-EXPANSION FACTOR IN ";A$(P4);" DIR'N = ";
1320     INPUT F1
1330     PRINT "GRID-EXPANSION FACTOR IN ";B$(P4);" DIR'N = ";
1340     INPUT F2
1350     IF F1><1 THEN D1=2*W1*(1-F1)/(1+F1-F1²(I1-2)-F1²(I1-1))
1360     IF F2><1 THEN D2=2*H1*(1-F2)/(1+F2-F2²(J1-2)-F2²(J1-1))
1370     IF ABS (F1 - 1)< = S9 THEN D1. = W1 / (I1 - 2)
1380     IF ABS (F2 - 1)< = S9 THEN D2 = H1 / (J1 - 2)
1390     Z(1) =  - D1 / 2
1400     R(1) =  - D2 / 2
1410      IF P4 > 0 THEN R(1) = R(1) + R1
1420      FOR I = 2 TO I1
1430         Z(I) = Z(I - 1) + D1
1440         D1 = F1 * D1
1450      NEXT I
1460      FOR J = 2 TO J1
1470         R(J) = R(J - 1) + D2
1480         D2 = D2 * F2
1490      NEXT J
1500  REM    INITIALISE O AND N ARRAYS
1510     PRINT "INITIAL (UNIFORM) TEMP (K OR C) = ";
1520     INPUT O(1,1)
1530     FOR J = 1 TO J1: FOR I = 1 TO I1
1540        O(I,J) = O(1,1)
1550        N(I,J) = O(1,1)
1560     NEXT I: NEXT J
1999     RETURN
```

In lines 1030–1040 a suitably small number (1E−10) is placed in S9, to be used in place of zero where necessary; likewise L9 is set to the 'very large' number 1E10. For some purposes these may be reset to 1E−30 and 1E30 respectively, but the settings chosen allow for S9 or L9 to be squared or cubed without disaster.

In line 1060 P3 is set to π: to ensure that this is appropriately accurate for the computer, the computer is allowed to calculate the value from the formula $\pi = 4 * \text{ARCTAN}(1)$.

In line 1080 the user is asked to select between plane and axi-symmetric geometry. The value of P4 (0 or 1 respectively) is used as the exponent of r^* in formulae such as (7.4). In lines 1090–1100 we provide for switching the labels between 'X' and 'Z': likewise between 'Y' and 'R' in lines 1130–1140. The number of nodes in the X (or Z) direction, I1, is set at 1120; the number of nodes in the Y (or R) direction is set at 1160. If the axi-symmetric option has been selected, the value of R1 (otherwise zero) is requested: this is the internal radius of the cylindrical annulus over which the problem is to be solved. The grid used by the THC program is shown in figure 8.2.

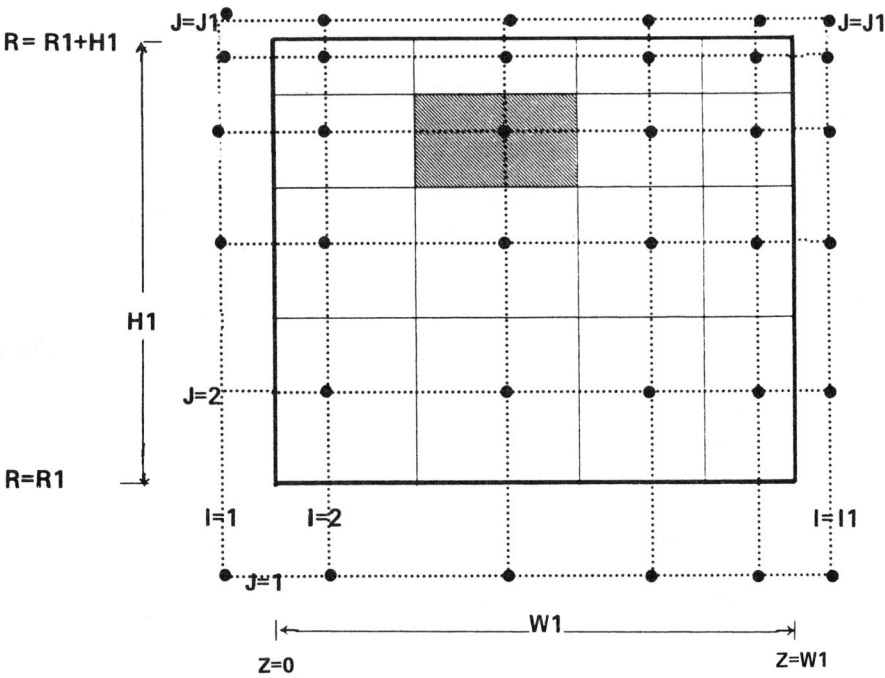

Figure 8.2 Thick lines denote the position of the physical edge of the calculation zone. Black dots denote nodes. Solid lines denote edges of cells. These are mid-way between nodes

The grid-expansion factors F1 and F2 are set in lines 1310–1340 and used in lines 1350–1360 which are implementations of expression (5.1). If the expansion factor is very close to unity, the initial value of the grid-spacing is obtained by dividing the length of the domain into $I1 - 2$ or $J1 - 2$ equal segments.

The variable $O(1, 1)$ is used to input a temperature which is then copied to the whole of the O and N arrays, thus serving as an initial temperature everywhere.

8.4 The PHYS Subroutine (2000-2999)

The variables introduced in the PHYS subroutine of THC are as follows

K0	2080	thermal conductivity of solid
K(I,J)	2100	thermal conductivity for cell (I,J)
A1,A2,A3,A4	2110-2150	(set in the EDGE subroutine)
W(I,J)	2180	thermal conductivity at WP for cell (I,J)
S(I,J)	2190	thermal conductivity at SP for cell (I,J)
R0	2220	density
C0	2230	specific heat capacity
Q(I,J)	2280	heat source for cell (I,J)

The thermal conductivity K0 is set and copied in K(I, J) to all the nodes in the body: if the conductivity is non-uniform, the values must be set at this point.

The formula (7.8) for the effective conductivity at the boundary, corresponding to the value h for the surface heat-transfer coefficient there, is implemented for each successive boundary (N, S, W, E) in lines 2110-2150, using the values of the surface heat-transfer coefficients A1, A3, A2 and A4 which will already have been set in the EDGE subroutine (see next section, 8.5).

In lines 2180-2190 the effective conductivities at the WP and SP nodes are calculated using formula (7.6) and stored in the W and S arrays. They are, in fact, divided by Dz and Dr respectively before storing – purely for convenience of calculation later on. The S array is then further multiplied by r in the case of axi-symmetric geometry, just as we explained, in the numerator of formula (7.4).

The density R0 and specific heat capacity C0 are set in lines 2220-2230. The heat sources at each node Q(I, J) are set in lines 2260-2290. This is assumed to be uniform but can be set non-uniform by modifying this part of the code.

The PHYS subroutine of the THC program (2000-2999) is

```
2000 REM   SUBROUTINE PHYS FOR PHYSICAL PARAMETERS
2010 REM   R0 IS DENSITY, C0 IS SPECIFIC HEAT CAPACITY, SI UNITS
2020 REM   W ARRAY STORES CONDUCTIVITY TO WEST OF NODE (K W-P)
2030 REM   S ARRAY STORES CONDUCTIVITY TO SOUTH OF NODE (K S-P)
2040 REM   W AND S ARRAYS DIVIDED BY CORRESPONDING DELTA-Z
2050 REM    K ARRAY STORES THERMAL CONDUCTIVITIES
2060 REM    NOTE K ARRAY CAN BE SACRIFICED, USING TIME-STEP
2070 REM    K0 IS THERMAL CONDUCTIVITY (MAY NOT BE UNIFORM)
2080 INPUT "THERMAL CONDUCTIVITY (W/mK) = ";K0
2090 FOR J = 1 TO J1
2095      FOR I = 1 TO I1
2100      K(I,J) = K0
2110      K(I,J1) = A1 * (R(J1) - R(J1 - 1)) / 2
2120      K(I,1) = A3 * (R(2) - R(1)) / 2
2130   NEXT I
2140   K(1,J) = A2 * (Z(2) - Z(1)) / 2
2150   K(I1,J) = A4 * (Z(I1) - Z(I1 - 1)) / 2
```

76   *Microcomputer Modelling by Finite Differences*

```
2160 NEXT J
2170 FOR J = 2 TO J1: FOR I = 2 TO I1
2180     W(I,J)=2*K(I-1,J)*K(I,J)/(K(I-1,J)+K(I,J))/(Z(I)-Z(I-1))
2190     S(I,J)=2*K(I,J-1)*K(I,J)/(K(I,J-1)+K(I,J))/(R(J)-R(J-1))
2200     IF P4 > 0 THEN S(I,J) = S(I,J) *(R(J)+R(J-1))/2
2210 NEXT I: NEXT J
2220 INPUT "DENSITY (kg/m²3) = ";RO
2230 INPUT "SPECIFIC HEAT (J/kgK) = ";CO
2240 REM     SET SOURCE IN Q ARRAY, DEFAULT IS 0
2250 PRINT "HEAT SOURCE (UNIFORM) =";
2260 INPUT Q(1,1)
2270 FOR J = 1 TO J1: FOR I = 1 TO I1
2280    Q(I,J) = Q(1,1)
2290 NEXT I: NEXT J
2999 RETURN
```

8.5 The EDGE Subroutine (3000-3999)

The variables introduced in the EDGE subroutine are

A1	3100	surface heat-transfer coefficient on North boundary
A2	3140	surface heat-transfer coefficient on West boundary
A3	3200	surface heat-transfer coefficient on South boundary
A4	3240	surface heat-transfer coefficient on East boundary
A6	3320	free-stream or surface temperature on North boundary
A7	3400	free-stream or surface temperature on West boundary
A8	3480	free-stream or surface temperature on South boundary
A9	3560	free-stream or surface temperature on East boundary

The surface heat-transfer coefficients A1, A2, A3, A4 are set for the N, W, E and S boundaries of the body.

The values of the temperatures along the north-most line of nodes (I, J1) are set via the variable A6. This is requested as the 'temp. of north boundary' or the 'free-stream temp. (north)' according to the value of the Biot number (or rather of the surface heat-transfer coefficient A1) on the north edge of the body (lines 3260-3300). Using the variables E$ and F$ (lines 3040-3060) the 'prompts' are switched to 'external' rather than 'north' if axi-symmetric geometry has been selected.

The variables A7, A8 and A9 are used in a similar way to A6, for the West, South and East boundaries respectively.

The routine thus provides explicitly for three common types of boundary condition (see chapter 7)

> fixed temperatures at any of the sides — by setting the coresponding heat-transfer coefficient to L9 (an 'infinite heat transfer rate')
> finite surface heat transfer rate — by setting the corresponding heat transfer coefficient to the value required

zero gradient, as at an axis of symmetry or a perfectly insulated boundary ('adiabatic' condition) — by setting the heat transfer coefficient to S9 ('zero heat transfer rate').

Though the phantom nodes ($I = 1$, $I = I1$, $J = 1$, $J = J1$) are used all the way round the boundary of the solid to store the 'free-stream' values of the temperatures, the values printed out in PLOT for the boundaries are the correctly interpolated values (using Ohm's Law: formula (7.7)) for the physical edges and not the free-stream values.

The EDGE subroutine of the THC program (3000-3999) is

```
3000    REM EDGE SUBROUTINE FOR BOUNDARY CONDITIONS
3020    PRINT "SURFACE HEAT TRANSFER COEFFS.(J/m²2K)"
3040    IF P4 = 1 THEN E$ = "EXTERNAL"
3050    IF P4 = 1 THEN F$ = "INTERNAL"
3060    IF P4 = 0 THEN E$ = "NORTH"
3070    IF P4 = 0 THEN F$ = "SOUTH"
3080    PRINT E$;" BOUNDARY =";
3100    INPUT A1
3120    PRINT "WEST BOUNDARY =";
3140    INPUT A2
3160    IF P4 = 0 OR R1 <> 0 THEN 3180
3165        A3 = S9
3170    GOTO 3220
3180    PRINT F$;" BOUNDARY =";
3200    INPUT A3
3220    PRINT "EAST BOUNDARY =";
3240    INPUT A4
3260    IF A1<1E-5 THEN 3340
3280    IF A1<1E6 THEN PRINT "FREE-STREAM TEMP (";E$;") IN K OR C = ";
3300    IF A1>=1E6 THEN PRINT "TEMP OF ";E$;" BOUNDARY (K OR C) = ";
3320    INPUT A6
3340    IF A2<1E-5 THEN 3420
3360    IF A2<1E6 THEN PRINT "FREE-STREAM TEMP (WEST) IN K OR C = ";
3380    IF A2>=1E6 THEN PRINT "TEMP OF WEST BOUNDARY (K OR C) = ";
3400    INPUT A7
3420    IF A3<1E-5 THEN 3500
3440    IF A3<1E6 THEN PRINT "FREE-STREAM TEMP (";F$;") IN K OR C = ";
3460    IF A3>=1E6 THEN PRINT "TEMP OF ";F$;" BOUNDARY (K OR C) = ";
3480    INPUT A8
3500    IF A4<1E-5 THEN 3580
3520    IF A4<1E6 THEN PRINT "FREE-STREAM TEMP (EAST) IN K OR C= ";
3540    IF A4>=1E6 THEN PRINT "TEMP OF EAST BOUNDARY (K OR C)= ";
3560    INPUT A9
3580    FOR J = 1 TO J1
3600        FOR I = 1 TO I1
3620            IF J = J1 THEN N(I,J) = A6
3640            IF I = 1 THEN N(I,J) = A7
3660            IF J = 1 THEN N(I,J) = A8
```

78   *Microcomputer Modelling by Finite Differences*

```
3680            IF I = I1 THEN N(I,J) = A9
3700      NEXT I
3720 NEXT J
3999 RETURN
```

8.6 The WORK Subroutine (4000-4999)

The variables used in WORK are

C3	4030	counter for iterations
N3	4050	maximum number of iterations at a given time
N4	4080	I subscript of node used for monitoring temperatures
N5	4090	J subscript of node used for monitoring temperatures
T3	4100	$\rho\, c_V\,/\mathrm{D}t$
D3	4110	residual
R6	4170	r* (i.e. either 1 or r)
R3	4190	r*.Dr
Z3	4220	Dz
A(I)	4230	TDMA coefficient
B(I)	4240	TDMA coefficient
C(I)	4250	TDMA coefficient
D(I)	4260	TDMA coefficient
M1	4320	A(I)/D(I-1)
O	4380	value of temperature before current iteration began
D4	4460	change in temperature in the current time-step

On entering the WORK subroutine, the iteration counter C3 is set to zero (line 4030). Then a check is made (line 4040) as to whether this is not the first time-step: the test is whether t is greater than $\mathrm{D}t$ (T1 > T2). If not, the maximum number N7 of iterations that will be allowed at any given time (after which it is reasonable to guess that the process is not converging) is set to 200 (line 4060). In lines 4080-4090 the 'monitoring location' (I = N4, J = N5) is selected arbitrarily to be at the centre of the grid.

At line 4100 (for all times) the value of $\rho\, c_V/\mathrm{D}t$ is stored for convenience of calculation.

The equations we actually have to solve are (see expressions (7.3) and (7.4)) the finite-difference form of equation (6.1).

$$\frac{k_{\mathrm{PE}}\dfrac{T_{\mathrm{E}}^+ - T_{\mathrm{P}}^+}{z_{\mathrm{E}} - z_{\mathrm{P}}} - k_{\mathrm{WP}}\dfrac{T_{\mathrm{P}}^+ - T_{\mathrm{W}}^+}{z_{\mathrm{P}} - z_{\mathrm{W}}}}{z_{\mathrm{PE}} - z_{\mathrm{WP}}} +$$

The THC (Transient Heat Conduction) Computer Program

$$+ \frac{1}{r_P^*} \frac{k_{PN} r_{PN}^* \dfrac{T_N^+ - T_P^+}{r_N - r_P} - k_{SP} r_{SP}^* \dfrac{T_P^+ - T_S^+}{r_P - r_S}}{r_{PN} - r_{SP}}$$

$$= \rho\, c_v \frac{T_P^+ - T_P^-}{Dt} - S \tag{8.1}$$

which we must rearrange to make T_P^+ (that is, N(I, J)) the subject.

If we use the BASIC names for the variables, we can write (8.1) as

```
(W(I+1,J)*(N(I+1,J)-N(I,J))  -  W(I,J)*(N(I,J)-N(I-1,J)))  / Z3
+
(S(I,J+1)*(N(I,J+1)-N(I,J))  -  S(I,J)*(N(I,J)-N(I,J-1)))  / R3
=
T3*(N(I,J)-O(I,J))  -  Q(I,J)
```
(8.2)

So we can now see why we stored the W and S arrays ready-divided by Dz and Dr respectively, and why we defined T3 as we did (line 4100).

We can rearrange (8.2) to give an equation similar to

```
G4*Y(I) = G1*Y(I+1) +G2*Y(I-1) + G3
```
(2.10)

for N(I, J) in terms of all the other quantities

```
(W(I+1,J)/Z3 + W(I,J)/Z3 + S(I,J+1)/R3 + S(I,J)/R3 + T3) * N(I,J)
=
(W(I+1,J)/Z3) * N(I+1,J) + (W(I,J)/Z3) * N(I-1,J)
+
S(I,J+1)*N(I,J+1)/R3 + S(I,J)*N(I,J-1)/R3 + T3*O(I,J) + Q(I,J)
```

So, if we put

```
G4 = (W(I+1,J)/Z3 + W(I,J)/Z3 + S(I,J+1)/R3 + S(I,J)/R3 + T3)
G1 = (W(I,J)/Z3)
G2 = (W(I+1,J)/Z3)
G3 = S(I,J+1)*N(I,J+1)/R3 + S(I,J)*N(I,J-1)/R3 + T3*O(I,J)+Q(I,J)
```

we can solve our equation by either point-iteration (as in chapter 2) or using the tri-diagonal matrix algorithm (chapter 4).

We have, in fact, cheated slightly by lumping all the ',J + 1)' and ',J − 1)' terms in with the constant, G3. This means that if we use the TDMA we are going to be assuming that — for the purposes of solving along the line with subscript J — the values of the temperatures are 'known' on lines J − 1 and J + 1. Of course, when we come to line J + 1, we shall correct the values on line J + 1. We shall be using the TDMA to give us at a single gulp the exact solutions of the finite-difference equations along the line $y = R(J)$, taking the values on the lines above and below it as known. Clearly, the process will have to involve iteration if the values are in fact not known but just 'the latest guess'. But at least we are not having to iterate point by point, just line by line. For typical problems, this makes the process about three times as fast.

It is important to arrange the problem so that the severe variations in temperature occur in the I direction, as this is the direction of the TDMA. In the extreme case, if the problem is in fact one-dimensional, the TDMA will solve it in one go if it is arranged so that the one dimension in which changes occur lies along the direction of the TDMA, while even with the TDMA the problem will require iteration if it is arranged with the variations perpendicular to the direction of the TDMA.

Convergence will be made faster even for two-dimensional problems if the greatest variations can be made to lie in the direction in which the TDMA operates. One point to note is that in the direction of the TDMA (here it is the I direction) there must be at least four nodes: there have to be at least three in the other direction.

Exercise 8.1

Explain why the THC program will fail if I1 < 4 or if J1 < 3.
(*Clue:* see lines 4370 and 4160.)

As in chapter 4, if we write

G1	as	C(I)
G2	as	A(I)
G3	as	−B(I)
G4	as	−D(I)

we can use the TDMA exactly as in chapter 4. This is done in lines 4200 to 4480.

The changes in the values of the temperatures are monitored by accumulating the changes normalised as suggested in chapter 3 by dividing by the previous values of the temperatures at the same nodes (in fact the values are simultaneously stabilised by using the average of the previous and current values of the temperature in the denominator). The test for convergence is made by comparing the sum D3 of these changes with the value of the convergence criterion C2 set in line 170, where again we have followed the suggestion made in chapter 3 that we should take account of the number of nodes in the whole grid when assessing convergence. The formula for C2 ensures that it is proportional to $(I1 - 2) * (J1 - 2)$, the number of nodes within the body.

The 'monitoring location' (I = N4, J = N5), placed during the first time-step in lines 4080–4090 at the centre of the grid, is reset to be at the node where there is the greatest change in temperature since the last time-step. This device has the effect of ensuring that the values printed out at each iteration are the

… ones of greatest significance and that the degree of (pseudo-)convergence displayed is the 'worst' currently achieved.

The sweep over, the value of C3 is increased by one, a check made to see whether C3 is an integral multiple of N7, and hence whether convergence information is required. If it is required, the information is printed (C3, T1, N4, N5, N(N4, N5), D3). If D3 remains above C2 the iteration is completed. Otherwise control is returned to MAIN.

If the number of iterations exceeds N3, set to 200 in line 4060, the solution procedure is terminated and the unconverged solutions printed out by a call to subroutine PLOT (GOSUB 5000).

The WORK subroutine is illustrated in figure 8.3: for simplicity, this shows the 'point-iteration' procedure rather than the TDMA.

The WORK subroutine of the THC program (4000-4999) is

```
4000    REM     SUBROUTINE WORK FOR CALCULATIONS
4010    REM     MODIFIED TO USE TDMA
4020    REM     C3 IS THE COUNTER USED FOR ITERATIONS
4030        C3 = 0
4040         IF T1>T2 THEN 4100
4050    REM N3 IS THE MAX PERMITTED £ OF ITERATIONS AT A GIVEN TIME
4060        N3 = 200
4070    REM     N(N4,N5) IS THE MONITORING AND CONVERGENCE CHECK POINT
4080        N4 = INT ((I1 + 1) / 2)
4090        N5 = INT ((J1 + 1) / 2)
4100        T3 = R0 * C0 / T2
4110        D3 = 0
4120         IF C3>N3 THEN 4560
4130    REM
4140    REM     HERE WE START TO SWEEP THE LINES
4150    REM
4160        FOR J = 2 TO J1 - 1
4170            R6 = 1
4180            IF P4>0 THEN R6 = R(J)
4190            R3 = (R(J + 1) - R(J - 1)) / 2 * R6
4200            REM     HERE WE USE THE TDMA ALONG A LINE
4210            FOR I = 2 TO I1 - 1
4220                Z3 = (Z(I + 1) - Z(I - 1)) / 2: REM    Z3 IS DZ
4230                A(I) = W(I,J) / Z3
4240                B(I)=-T3*O(I,J)-Q(I,J)-(S(I,J+1)*N(I,J+1)
                        +S(I,J)*N(I,J-1))/R3
4250                C(I) = W(I + 1,J) / Z3
4260                D(I) = - T3 - (W(I,J)+W(I+1,J))/Z3
                        -(S(I,J)+S(I,J+1))/R3
4270            NEXT I
4280            B(2) = B(2) - A(2) * N(1,J)
4290            B(I1 - 1) = B(I1 - 1) - C(I1 - 1) * N(I1,J)
4300            FOR I = 3 TO I1 - 1
4310                REM    MODIFY THE D(I) AND B(I)
4320                M1 = A(I) / D(I - 1)
4330                D(I) = D(I) - M1 * C(I - 1)
4340                B(I) = B(I) - M1 * B(I - 1)
```

```
4350            NEXT I
4360            N(I1 - 1,J) = B(I1 - 1) / D(I1 - 1)
4370            FOR I = I1 - 2 TO 2 STEP - 1
4380              O = N(I,J)
4390              N(I,J) = (B(I) - C(I) * N(I + 1,J)) / D(I)
4400              REM HERE WE ARE RECOVERING THE NEW TEMPERATURES
4410              REM    HAVING STORED EACH OLD TEMPERATURE IN O
4420              REM    D3 IS GLOBAL CHANGE IN N OVER THE ITERATION
4430            D3 = D3 + ABS(O-N(I,J))*2/(ABS(O)+ABS(N(I,J))+.001)
4440              IF C3>0 THEN 4480
4450              REM NOW DETERMINE MAX DN/DT AND MONITOR THIS UFN
4460              D4 = ABS (N(I,J) - O(I,J))
4470              IF D4>D5 THEN N4 = I
4472              IF D4>D5 THEN N5 = J
4474              IF D4>D5 THEN D5 = D4
4480            NEXT I
4485          NEXT J
4490          C3 = C3 + 1
4500          REM   CHECK IF PRINTOUT REQUIRED AT THIS ITERATION
4510          IF C3 / N7>< INT (C3 / N7) THEN 4540
4520          PRINT C3;" SWEEPS AT ";T1;" S GIVE N(";
4525          PRINT N4;",";N5;")= ";N(N4,N5);
4530          PRINT "; CHANGE= ";D3
4540          IF D3>C2 THEN 4110
4550          RETURN
4560          PRINT N3;" ITERATIONS DID NOT ENSURE CONVERGENCE"
4570          PRINT "THE FOLLOWING RESULTS ARE UNCONVERGED"
4580          GOSUB 5000
4590          STOP
4999   REM  TERMINATE HERE IF UNCONVERGED.
```

8.7 The PLOT Subroutine (5000–5999) and the DRAW Subroutine (9000–9999)

These routines do not contain much that you have to understand at this stage: you are unlikely to need to modify them before covering the material in the rest of the book. Essentially, the routine PLOT is similar to the PLOT routine of Program 7, except that it now provides contour plots of the temperatures (isothermals) rather than a graph of temperature against distance. The DRAW routines are identical to those of Program 7. For this reason, so as not to burden you with too much detail at this point, the listing of PLOT has been relegated to the appendix, which also contains a full sequential listing of the THC program. There is absolutely no reason why you should not peep at the appendix now if you want to: it would not do you any harm.

Chapters 9 and 10 will describe applications of the THC program. For further applications you will then need to read the appendix, so that you can modify the output to your requirements.

The THC (Transient Heat Conduction) Computer Program

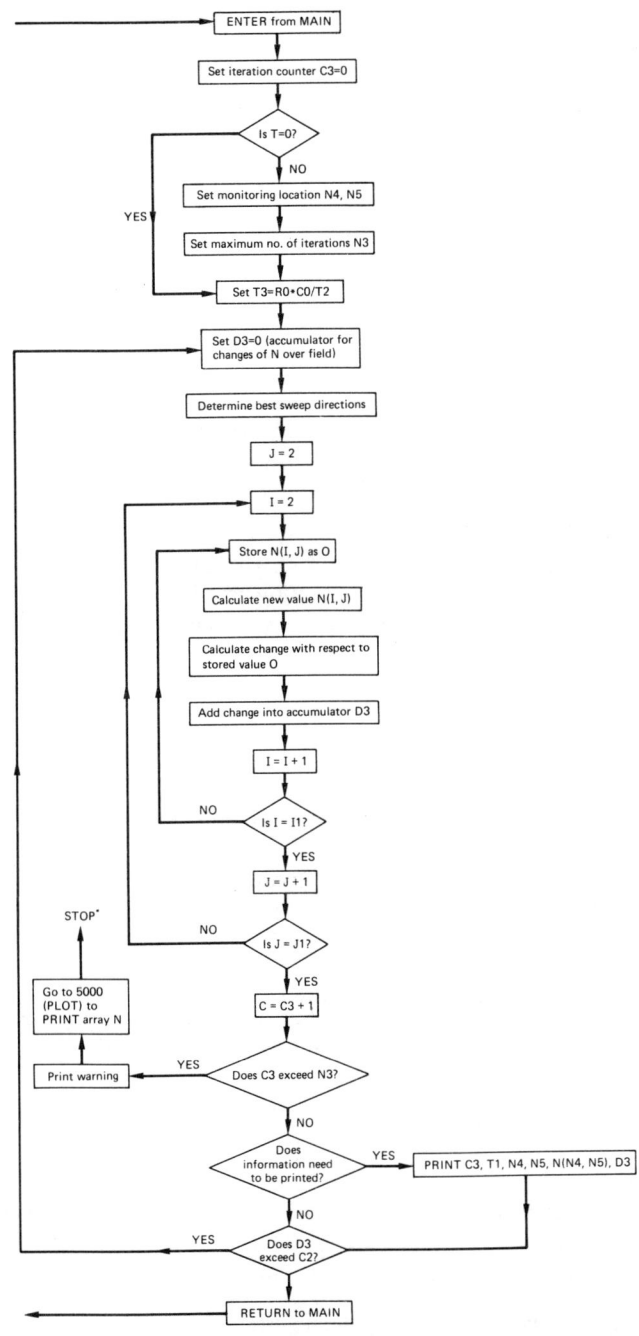

Figure 8.3 Flowchart of the WORK subroutine (4000–4999)

9 Elementary Applications of the THC Program

9.1 Introduction

By 'elementary' applications we mean problems that can be solved using the THC program described in chapter 8 exactly as it stands. Some of the applications described here are far from trivial — many of them could not be solved in a reasonable time except by using a computer.

The examples given are just a sample of what can be done with the THC program: you will be able to devise other problems for it to solve. At the end of this chapter are examples of what happens when you RUN the program for various cases.

9.2 One-dimensional Problems

9.2.1 Fixed temperatures at two ends of an insulated bar (RUN 9.1)

Consider a bar of length 1 metre, which is initially at 20° Celsius, suddenly heated at one end to 100° Celsius, while the other end is maintained at 20° Celsius. Figure 9.1 shows the set-up.

Figure 9.1

If the bar is insulated along its length, the problem is one-dimensional. Obtain the temperatures at 500 seconds for a stainless steel bar (R0 = 7850, C0 = 460, K0 = 52). Compare the results you get

      for time-steps of 50 seconds and a grid of I1 = 12, J1 = 3 (RUN 9.1)
      for a single time-step of 500 seconds using the same grid
      for a time-step of 1E6 seconds (that is, to a thoroughly steady state)
      for a copper bar (R0 = 8960, C0 = 380, K0 = 390) at 500 s using 50 s steps

Remember to align the problem with the TDMA — that is, along the West-East lines. Set the N and S boundaries to be adiabatic and the W and E ones to be fixed-temperature boundaries with temperatures as given.

Using the definition of Fourier number

```
F = K0*T1/(R0*C0*L*L)
```

calculate the Fourier number F corresponding to 500 seconds for the steel bar. Then calculate the number of seconds (T1) corresponding to F for a copper bar and use THC to calculate the temperatures for the copper bar at F. Check that the values are in fact the same as those for the steel bar at the same value of F (or explain any differences).

Next, change the end boundary condition for the steel bar from being fixed at room temperature to being adiabatic (insulated). Does it change the results at 500 seconds? At 1E6 seconds?

9.2.2 Fully-developed laminar flow between parallel plates (Couette flow) (RUN 9.2)

The equation for flow between parallel plates is

$$\nabla \cdot (\mu \nabla U) = dp/dz$$

So if we understand

	for	
U		T
μ		k
$-dp/dz$		S

we shall be able to use THC to obtain the solutions. We shall have to set the 'temperatures' (actually velocities) to zero at the two ends to satisfy the no-slip boundary condition (figure 9.2). The time-step will be 1E6 to ensure steady state.

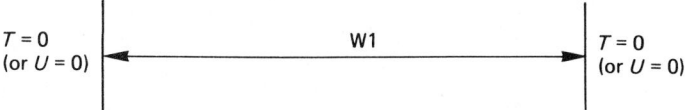

Figure 9.2

Again, align the problem West-East. (Try it N-S and see how long it takes to get a solution!).

Use 12 nodes E-W, 3 N-S and set the pressure-gradient to −100 — that is, the source = 100 — and K0 = 1. You should get a parabola (RUN 9.2).

Set the width equal to 1 metre (the distance between the plates). Check the result against what you would get using 7 nodes, an adiabatic East wall and width 0.5.

9.2.3 Flow in a circular pipe (Poiseuille flow) (RUN 9.3)

If we consider the fully developed flow in a circular pipe, we shall have to align the problem N–S, so that it will not take advantage of the TDMA as it stands. However, we may realign the TDMA N–S by using the following modifications to THC

```
4140  REM    HERE WE START TO SWEEP THE LINES
4150  REM
4160  FOR I = 2 TO I1 - 1
4170    Z3 = (Z(I + 1) - Z(I - 1)) / 2: REM    Z3 IS DZ
4180  REM    HERE WE USE THE TDMA ALONG A LINE
4190    FOR J = 2 TO J1 - 1
4200      R6 = 1
4210      IF P4 > 0 THEN R6 = R(J)
4220      R3 = (R(J + 1) - R(J - 1)) / 2 * R6
4230      A(J) = S(I,J) / R3
4240      B(J) = -T3*O(I,J)-Q(I,J)
                 -(W(I+1,J)*N(I+1,J)+W(I,J)*N(I-1,J))/Z3
4250      C(J) = S(I,J+1) / R3
4260      D(J)=-T3-(S(I,J)+S(I,J+1))/R3-(W(I,J)+W(I+1,J))/Z3
4270    NEXT J
4280    B(2) = B(2) - A(2) * N(I,1)
4290    B(J1 - 1) = B(J1 - 1) - C(J1 - 1) * N(I,J1)
4300    FOR J = 3 TO J1 - 1
4310      REM  MODIFY THE D(J) AND B(J)
4320      M1 = A(J) / D(J - 1)
4330      D(J) = D(J) - M1 * C(J - 1)
4340      B(J) = B(J) - M1 * B(J - 1)
4350    NEXT J
4360    N(I,J - 1) = B(J1 - 1) / D(J1 - 1)
4370    FOR J = I1 - 2 TO 2 STEP - 1
4380      O = N(I,J)
4390      N(I,J) = (B(J) - C(J) * N(I,J + 1)) / D(J)
4400      REM    HERE WE ARE RECOVERING THE NEW TEMPERATURES
4410      REM    HAVING STORED EACH OLD TEMPERATURE IN O
4420      REM    D3 IS GLOBAL CHANGE IN N OVER THE ITERATION
4430      D3 =D3+ABS(O-N(I,J))*2/(ABS(O)+ABS(N(I,J))+.001)
4440      IF C3 > 0 THEN 4480
4450      REM   NOW DETERMINE MAX DN/DT AND MONITOR THIS II.F.N.
4460      D4 = ABS (N(I,J) - O(I,J))
4470      IF D4 > D5 THEN N4 = I
4472      IF D4 > D5 THEN N5 = J
4474      IF D4 > D5 THEN D5 = D4
4480    NEXT J
4485  NEXT I
```

We have displayed the whole of the modified TDMA chunk of the WORK routine (4000-4999) to make it easy to see how we have flipped the I's and J's.

Select the axi-symmetric option of THC and set I1 = 3, J1 = 12, R1 = 0 and H1 = 1 (as this is a one-dimensional problem and aligned N–S, W1 can take any value you like). With the external 'temperature' set to zero, K0 = 1 and the 'heat source' set to 100, we shall get another parabola — with a different shape from that for Couette flow.

9.2.4 The distribution of heat in an annular cylinder (RUNs 9.4 and 9.5)

By setting R1 (the internal radius) to a value other than zero (take R1 = 1, say) with

```
I1 =     3
J1 =    12
W1 =     1
H1 =     1
F2 =   0.8
A1 = 1e10
A2 =1e-10
A3 = 1e10
A4 =1e-10
T2 =   1e6
no heat source
external temperature 100
internal temperature   0
```

we get the distribution of heat in an 'infinite' cylindrical annulus (figure 9.3) with internal radius 1 metre, external radius 2 metres (RUN 9.4). It is not really worthwhile asking for a contour plot, as this will (or should!) consist of parallel straight lines.

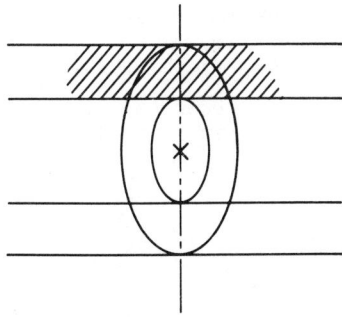

Figure 9.3

The analytical solution is

$$T = T_{in} + (T_{out} - T_{in}) * \ln(r/r_{in})/\ln(r_{out}/r_{in})$$

where 'in' and 'out' refer to the inner and outer walls of the cylindrical annulus.

Check this value for one point. You should find splendid agreement if you use a grid with 12 nodes.

The solutions are also those of the problem of finding the electric potential in the region between two concentric cylindrical shell conductors, the outer one held at 100 volts and the inner one grounded (that is, held at zero volts).

Now try an internal-boundary temperature of 20° Celsius (RUN 9.5).

9.2.5 Cylindrical annulus with heat source (RUN 9.6)

If we modify the specification of section 9.2.4 as follows

> internal and external faces both held at 0° Celsius
> a uniform heat source of 100

we shall get the profile of temperature in a cylindrical annulus with a heat source. Alternatively we may regard the solution as that for a fully-developed laminar flow in the region between two concentric cylinders (RUN 9.6).

If you set the internal radius R1 to 99 and use a uniform grid you should get good agreement with the Couette flow. Why? (Check section 7.1 for the answer.)

9.3 Two-dimensional Problems

9.3.1 The superposition principle (RUN 9.7)

Because the equation

$$\nabla \cdot (k \nabla T) = \rho c_v \, \partial T / \partial t - S$$

is 'linear' — it contains just linear functions of T and its derivatives (that is, no products of T's and derivatives) — we can take two solutions of the equation, add them together and obtain a third solution of the equation. To show that this is true, let us consider a square-sectioned block of steel, 1 metre wide and 1 metre high. R0 = 7850, C0 = 460, K0 = 52. Investigate the solutions for a 7 × 7 grid after 500 seconds in steps of 50 seconds (RUN 9.7) and 5000 seconds,

(a) with 100° imposed on the N face, the remaining faces being held at 0° (figure 9.4a)
(b) with 100° on the W face, zero on the others (figure 9.4b)
(c) with 100° on both N and W faces, zero on the other two (figure 9.4c).

If we are right, the results for (c) should be the sum of those for (a) and (b). Check this.

If we put 100° on the S face, zero on the rest, the problem will be solved slightly faster than in case (a). This is not just chance: it is because the iterations go from J = 2 to J = J1 − 1 − that is, from S to N (see figure 8.2). As a result, the information about the changes (at the suddenly-heated boundary) is being carried forward into regions where they are being felt (in the rest of the domain). It is exactly the same problem as spreading muck over your garden. You start

Elementary Applications of the THC Program 89

from the end of the garden where the muck is — not the far end. So we do not start at the unheated end of the domain when we want to spread the heat around, because it takes that much longer.

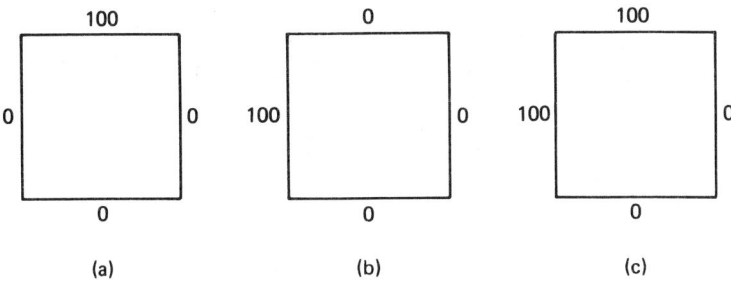

Figure 9.4

The contour plots will show roughly what is going on. Ignore the corners, as they are actually not part of our solution domain. If you think about it, we could set any of the corner values to any value we like and our solution procedure would ignore them. So, conversely, even if we know the values near them (just inside the body), we have no way of knowing what the corner values are. Common sense tells us that they are likely to be between the values on either side of them and this is what we have assumed. But if the N face is at 100° and the E face is at 0° what is the value at the NE corner: 100°, 0° or 50°? Our program takes the value as 50°, but the 'idealised' model used traditionally for analytical ('exact') solutions assumes that it is simultaneously 100° (when it is pretending to be part of the N face) and 0° (when it is being part of the E face). Which is just another example of the idiocies we have to put up with when we try to solve such problems 'exactly' (see, for example, figure 9.7 below).

The contours are drawn to lie at intervals of 0.1 ∗ (highest value − lowest value), so that they do not represent the same levels in two different contour plots unless the maximum and minimum values are the same.

9.3.2 Fully-developed laminar flow in a rectangular-sectioned duct

If we set the boundary values to zero on all four edges, set the source to 100 and go straight to steady state, with width and height equal to 1, we get the velocities of a fluid in a square-sectioned duct, 1 metre square, subject to a uniform pressure-gradient. We can improve the accuracy of our procedure if we use a 12 × 12 grid to examine the top-left quadrant (or any of the others), as the other three quarters are just copies of this, by symmetry. We get the results in figure 9.5. The corners are correct as the values are the same (zero) on either side of them: this ceases to be true as soon as we quarter the problem, as three of the corners would not know which face to belong to.

Now let the width increase from 1 to 2 ... 5 successively. Compare the results with those for the Couette flow and explain what is happening (see figures 9.5 and 9.6).

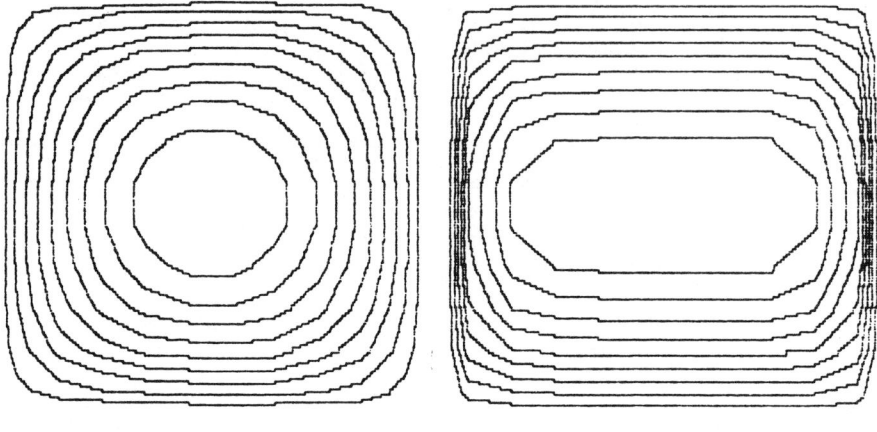

Figure 9.5 Width = 1   *Figure 9.6* Width = 5

9.3.3 The electric potential inside an infinite box

If we take the solutions of the problem in section 9.3.1 for steady state, preferably with a 12 × 12 grid, taking advantage of any symmetry of the problem, our contour plot will give us the equipotential lines for the region inside a box with one face held at 100 volts and the others at 0 volts.

Figure 9.7 shows the contour plot that we should get.

Spurious contours (see section 9.3.1)

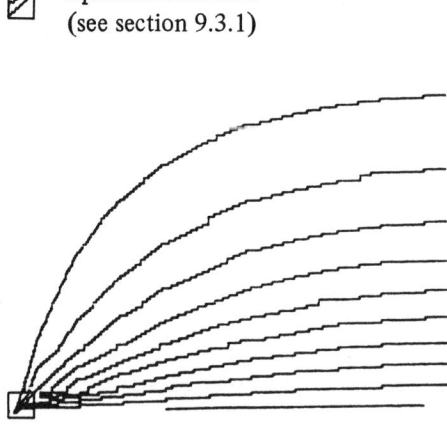

Figure 9.7

Elementary Applications of the THC Program   91

```
PLANE GEOMETRY (0) OR AXISYMMETRIC (1) 0
NO.OF NODES IN X DIR'N = ?12
NO.OF NODES IN Y DIR'N = ?3
HEIGHT (IN METRES) = ?1
WIDTH (IN METRES) = ?1
GRID-EXPANSION FACTOR IN X DIR'N = ?1
GRID-EXPANSION FACTOR IN Y DIR'N = ?1
INITIAL (UNIFORM) TEMP (K OR C) = ?20
SURFACE HEAT TRANSFER COEFFS.(J/m^2K)
NORTH BOUNDARY =?1E-10
WEST BOUNDARY =?1E10
SOUTH BOUNDARY =?1E-10
EAST BOUNDARY =?1E10
TEMP OF WEST BOUNDARY (K OR C) = ?100
TEMP OF EAST BOUNDARY (K OR C)= ?20
THERMAL CONDUCTIVITY (W/mK) = 52
DENSITY (kg/m^3) = 7850
SPECIFIC HEAT (J/kgK) = 460
HEAT SOURCE (UNIFORM) =?0
ENTER INITIAL TIME STEP ?50
ENTER FACTOR BY WHICH TIME-STEP IS TO BE ALTERED AT EACH STEP ?1

TIME OF NEXT DETAILED PRINTOUT ?500
1 SWEEPS AT  50 S GIVE N(2,2)= 29.5095039; CHANGE= .415765537
2 SWEEPS AT  50 S GIVE N(2,2)= 29.5095039; CHANGE= 0
1 SWEEPS AT 100 S GIVE N(2,2)= 37.3906165; CHANGE= .289615708



2 SWEEPS AT 450 S GIVE N(2,2)= 66.4601159; CHANGE= 0
1 SWEEPS AT 500 S GIVE N(2,2)= 68.5434839; CHANGE= .115421823
2 SWEEPS AT 500 S GIVE N(2,2)= 68.5434839; CHANGE= 0


   TEMPERATURE   DISTRIBUTION AFTER 500 SECONDS


    X=   0    .05  .15  .25  .35  .45  .55  .65  .75  .85  .95  1

Y=1       **  68.5 34.5 23.4 20.6 20.1 20.0 20.0 20.0 20.0 20.0 **
Y=.5     99.9 68.5 34.5 23.4 20.6 20.1 20.0 20.0 20.0 20.0 20.0 20
Y=0       **  68.5 34.5 23.4 20.6 20.1 20.0 20.0 20.0 20.0 20.0 **

MAX=99.9999967  MIN=20
```

RUN 9.1

```
PLANE GEOMETRY (0) OR AXISYMMETRIC (1) 0
NO.OF NODES IN X DIR'N = ?12
NO.OF NODES IN Y DIR'N = ?3
HEIGHT (IN METRES) = ?1
WIDTH (IN METRES) = ?1
GRID-EXPANSION FACTOR IN X DIR'N = ?1
GRID-EXPANSION FACTOR IN Y DIR'N = ?1
INITIAL (UNIFORM) TEMP (K OR C) = ?0
SURFACE HEAT TRANSFER COEFFS.(J/m^2K)
NORTH BOUNDARY =?1E-10
WEST BOUNDARY =?1E10
SOUTH BOUNDARY =?1E-10
EAST BOUNDARY =?1E10
TEMP OF WEST BOUNDARY (K OR C) = ?0
TEMP OF EAST BOUNDARY (K OR C)= ?0
THERMAL CONDUCTIVITY (W/mK) = 1
DENSITY (kg/m^3) = 1
SPECIFIC HEAT (J/kgK) = 1
HEAT SOURCE (UNIFORM) =?100
ENTER INITIAL TIME STEP ?1E6




      TEMPERATURE   DISTRIBUTION AFTER 1000000 SECONDS


     X=  0    .05  .15  .25  .35  .45  .55  .65  .75  .85  .95  1

 Y=1      **   2.49 6.49 9.49 11.4 12.4 12.4 11.4 9.49 6.49 2.49 **
 Y=.5    4E-8 2.49 6.49 9.49 11.4 12.4 12.4 11.4 9.49 6.49 2.49 4E-8
 Y=0      **   2.49 6.49 9.49 11.4 12.4 12.4 11.4 9.49 6.49 2.49 **

MAX=12.4999987   MIN=4.99999957E-09
STEADY-STATE REQUESTED
```

RUN 9.2

```
PLANE GEOMETRY (0) OR AXISYMMETRIC (1) 1
NO.OF NODES IN Z DIR'N = ?3
NO.OF NODES IN R DIR'N = ?7
INTERNAL RADIUS IN METRES (0 FOR SOLID  CYLINDER ) = ?0
RADIAL THICKNESS (IN METRES) = ?.5
LENGTH OF CYLINDER (IN METRES) = ?1
GRID-EXPANSION FACTOR IN Z DIR'N = ?1
GRID-EXPANSION FACTOR IN R DIR'N = ?1
INITIAL (UNIFORM) TEMP (K OR C) = ?0
SURFACE HEAT TRANSFER COEFFS.(J/m^2K)
EXTERNAL BOUNDARY =?1E10
WEST BOUNDARY =?1E-10
EAST BOUNDARY =?1E-10
TEMP OF EXTERNAL BOUNDARY (K OR C) = ?0
THERMAL CONDUCTIVITY (W/mK) = 1
DENSITY (kg/m^3) = 1
SPECIFIC HEAT (J/kgK) = 1
HEAT SOURCE (UNIFORM) =?100
ENTER INITIAL TIME STEP ?1E6
```

```
              TEMPERATURE   DISTRIBUTION AFTER 1000000 SECONDS

                      Z=  0    .5   1

                R=.5    **  2E-8  **
                R=.45  1.24 1.24 1.24
                R=.35  3.24 3.24 3.24
                R=.25  4.74 4.74 4.74
                R=.15  5.74 5.74 5.74
                R=.05  6.24 6.24 6.24
                R=0     **  6.24  **

              MAX=6.24999971   MIN=2.49999992E-09
```

RUN 9.3

```
PLANE GEOMETRY (0) OR AXISYMMETRIC (1) 1
NO.OF NODES IN Z DIR'N = ?3
NO.OF NODES IN R DIR'N = ?12
INTERNAL RADIUS IN METRES (0 FOR SOLID  CYLINDER ) = ?1
RADIAL THICKNESS (IN METRES) = ?1
LENGTH OF CYLINDER (IN METRES) = ?1
GRID-EXPANSION FACTOR IN Z DIR'N = ?1
GRID-EXPANSION FACTOR IN R DIR'N = ?0.8
INITIAL (UNIFORM) TEMP (K OR C) = ?0
SURFACE HEAT TRANSFER COEFFS.(J/m^2K)
EXTERNAL BOUNDARY =?1E10
WEST BOUNDARY =?1E-10
INTERNAL BOUNDARY =?1E10
EAST BOUNDARY =?1E-10
TEMP OF EXTERNAL BOUNDARY (K OR C) = ?100
TEMP OF INTERNAL BOUNDARY (K OR C) = ?0
THERMAL CONDUCTIVITY (W/mK) = 1
DENSITY (kg/m^3) = 1
SPECIFIC HEAT (J/kgK) = 1
HEAT SOURCE (UNIFORM) =?0
ENTER INITIAL TIME STEP ?1E6


          TEMPERATURE  DISTRIBUTION AFTER 1000000 SECONDS


                Z=  0     .5    1

               R=2      **   100   **
               R=1.98 99.0 99.0 99.0
               R=1.95 96.6 96.6 96.6
               R=1.91 93.5 93.5 93.5
               R=1.85 89.5 89.5 89.5
               R=1.79 84.4 84.4 84.4
               R=1.71 77.8 77.8 77.8
               R=1.61 69.0 69.0 69.0
               R=1.48 57.2 57.2 57.2
               R=1.32 41.0 41.0 41.0
               R=1.12 17.7 17.7 17.7
               R=1      **   1E-7  **

          MAX=100        MIN=1.42914303E-08
```

RUN 9.4

Elementary Applications of the THC Program 95

```
PLANE GEOMETRY (0) OR AXISYMMETRIC (1) 1
NO.OF NODES IN Z DIR'N = ?3
NO.OF NODES IN R DIR'N = ?12
INTERNAL RADIUS IN METRES (0 FOR SOLID  CYLINDER ) = ?1
RADIAL THICKNESS (IN METRES) = ?1
LENGTH OF CYLINDER (IN METRES) = ?1
GRID-EXPANSION FACTOR IN Z DIR'N = ?1
GRID-EXPANSION FACTOR IN R DIR'N = ?.8
INITIAL (UNIFORM) TEMP (K OR C) = ?20
SURFACE HEAT TRANSFER COEFFS.(J/m^2K)
EXTERNAL BOUNDARY =?1E10
WEST BOUNDARY =?1E-10
INTERNAL BOUNDARY =?1E10
EAST BOUNDARY =?1E-10
TEMP OF EXTERNAL BOUNDARY (K OR C) = ?100
TEMP OF INTERNAL BOUNDARY (K OR C) = ?20
THERMAL CONDUCTIVITY (W/mK) = 1
DENSITY (kg/m^3) = 1
SPECIFIC HEAT (J/kgK) = 1
HEAT SOURCE (UNIFORM) =?0
ENTER INITIAL TIME STEP ?1E6


              TEMPERATURE   DISTRIBUTION AFTER 1000000 SECONDS


                    Z=  0    .5    1

                    R=2     **   100   **
                    R=1.98 99.2 99.2 99.2
                    R=1.95 97.2 97.2 97.2
                    R=1.91 94.8 94.8 94.8
                    R=1.85 91.6 91.6 91.6
                    R=1.79 87.5 87.5 87.5
                    R=1.71 82.2 82.2 82.2
                    R=1.61 75.2 75.2 75.2
                    R=1.48 65.8 65.8 65.8
                    R=1.32 52.8 52.8 52.8
                    R=1.12 34.2 34.2 34.2
                    R=1      **  20    **

                    MAX=100        MIN=20
```

RUN 9.5

```
PLANE GEOMETRY (0) OR AXISYMMETRIC (1) 1
NO.OF NODES IN Z DIR'N = ?3
NO.OF NODES IN R DIR'N = ?12
INTERNAL RADIUS IN METRES (0 FOR SOLID  CYLINDER ) = ?1
RADIAL THICKNESS (IN METRES) = ?1
LENGTH OF CYLINDER (IN METRES) = ?1
GRID-EXPANSION FACTOR IN Z DIR'N = ?1
GRID-EXPANSION FACTOR IN R DIR'N = ?1
INITIAL (UNIFORM) TEMP (K OR C) = ?0
SURFACE HEAT TRANSFER COEFFS.(J/m^2K)
EXTERNAL BOUNDARY =?1E10
WEST BOUNDARY =?1E-10
INTERNAL BOUNDARY =?1E10
EAST BOUNDARY =?1E-10
TEMP OF EXTERNAL BOUNDARY (K OR C) = ?0
TEMP OF INTERNAL BOUNDARY (K OR C) = ?0
THERMAL CONDUCTIVITY (W/mK) = 1
DENSITY (kg/m^3) = 1
SPECIFIC HEAT (J/kgK) = 1
HEAT SOURCE (UNIFORM) =?100
ENTER INITIAL TIME STEP ?1E6


           TEMPERATURE   DISTRIBUTION AFTER 1000000 SECONDS


              Z=  0    .5   1

              R=2    **  4E-8 **
              R=1.95 2.29 2.29 2.29
              R=1.85 6.10 6.10 6.10
              R=1.75 9.10 9.10 9.10
              R=1.65 11.2 11.2 11.2
              R=1.55 12.4 12.4 12.4
              R=1.45 12.7 12.7 12.7
              R=1.35 12.0 12.0 12.0
              R=1.25 10.2 10.2 10.2
              R=1.15 7.23 7.23 7.23
              R=1.05 2.90 2.90 2.90
              R=1     **  5E-8 **

           MAX=12.7791962  MIN=4.59476098E-09
```

RUN 9.6

Elementary Applications of the THC Program

```
PLANE GEOMETRY (0) OR AXISYMMETRIC (1) 0
NO.OF NODES IN X DIR'N = ?7
NO.OF NODES IN Y DIR'N = ?7
HEIGHT (IN METRES) = ?1
WIDTH (IN METRES) = ?1
GRID-EXPANSION FACTOR IN X DIR'N = ?1
GRID-EXPANSION FACTOR IN Y DIR'N = ?1
INITIAL (UNIFORM) TEMP (K OR C) = ?0
SURFACE HEAT TRANSFER COEFFS.(J/m^2K)
NORTH BOUNDARY =?1E10
WEST BOUNDARY =?1E10
SOUTH BOUNDARY =?1E10
EAST BOUNDARY =?1E10
TEMP OF NORTH BOUNDARY (K OR C) = ?100
TEMP OF WEST BOUNDARY (K OR C) = ?0
TEMP OF SOUTH BOUNDARY (K OR C) = ?0
TEMP OF EAST BOUNDARY (K OR C)= ?0
THERMAL CONDUCTIVITY (W/mK) = 52
DENSITY (kg/m^3) = 7850
SPECIFIC HEAT (J/kgK) = 460
HEAT SOURCE (UNIFORM) =?0
ENTER INITIAL TIME STEP ?50
ENTER FACTOR BY WHICH TIME-STEP IS TO BE ALTERED AT EACH STEP ?1
          •
          •
          •
          •
    TEMPERATURE   DISTRIBUTION AFTER 500 SECONDS


    X=   0    .1    .3    .5    .7    .9    1
Y=1       **  99.9  99.9  99.9  99.9  99.9  **
Y=.9     1E-5 23.4  27.1  27.4  27.1  23.4  1E-5
Y=.7     1E-6 2.00  2.50  2.53  2.50  2.00  1E-6
Y=.5     6E-8 .129  .170  .173  .170  .129  6E-8
Y=.3     0    6E-2  9E-2  9E-2  9E-2  6E-2  0
Y=.1     0    3E-3  4E-3  4E-3  4E-3  3E-3  0
Y=0       **  0     0     0     0     0     **

MAX=99.9999962  MIN=0
```

RUN 9.7

10 Further Applications of the THC Program

10.1 Update to Allow for Further Modifications

As it stands, the THC program uses uniform initial temperatures, uniformly distributed heat sources and uniform conductivity. This is rather a shame as the method used nowhere assumes that these properties are uniform. We have, in fact, gone to great lengths to ensure that the program is designed to cope with non-uniform conductivity: this was the point of using an Ohm's Law approach to the combination of thermal resistances and hence of thermal conductivities (chapter 7). Because our solution procedure allows us to incorporate regions of effectively infinite or zero thermal conductivity, we should be able to 'paint' fixed-temperature or adiabatic boundaries within a solid and thus obtain solutions for bodies with quite complicated shapes.

A slight modification to the program will allow us to insert non-uniformities of the initial temperature distribution, the sources and the conductivities.

```
1500    REM     INITIALISE O AND N ARRAYS
1510      PRINT "INITIAL (UNIFORM) TEMP (K OR C) = ";
1520      INPUT O(1,1)
1530      FOR J = 1 TO J1: FOR I = 1 TO I1
1540        O(I,J) = O(1,1)
1550        N(I,J) = O(1,1)
1560      NEXT I: NEXT J
        1600 PRINT "ANY (FURTHER) NON-UNIFORMITIES? ";
        1610 INPUT A$
        1620 IF LEFT$(A$,1)<>"Y" THEN 1999
        1630 GOSUB 6000
        1640 FOR I=I8 TO I9:FOR J=J8 TO J9:
                O(I,J)=Q(1,1):N(I,J)=Q(1,1):
                NEXT J: NEXT I
        1650 GOTO 1600
1999      RETURN


2000    REM     SUBROUTINE PHYS FOR PHYSICAL PARAMETERS
2010    REM     R0 IS DENSITY, C0 IS SPECIFIC HEAT CAPACITY, SI UNITS
2020    REM     W ARRAY STORES CONDUCTIVITY TO WEST OF NODE (K P-W)
2030    REM     S ARRAY STORES CONDUCTIVITY TO SOUTH OF NODE (K P-S)
2040    REM     W AND S ARRAYS DIVIDED BY CORRESPONDING DELTA-Z
2050    REM     K ARRAY STORES THERMAL CONDUCTIVITIES
```

Further Applications of the THC Program

```
2060   REM    NOTE K ARRAY CAN BE SACRIFICED, USING TIME-STEP
2070   REM    K0 IS THERMAL CONDUCTIVITY (MAY NOT BE UNIFORM)
2080      INPUT "THERMAL CONDUCTIVITY (W/mK) = ";K0
2090      FOR J = 1 TO J1
2095         FOR I = 1 TO I1
2100            K(I,J) = K0
2110            K(I,J1) = A1 * (R(J1) - R(J1 - 1)) / 2
2120            K(I,1) = A3 * (R(2) - R(1)) / 2
2130         NEXT I
2140         K(1,J) = A2 * (Z(2) - Z(1)) / 2
2150         K(I1,J) = A4 * (Z(I1) - Z(I1 - 1)) / 2
2160      NEXT J
 2161 PRINT "ANY (FURTHER) NON-UNIFORMITIES? ";
 2162 INPUT A$
 2163 IF LEFT$(A$,1)<>"Y" THEN 2170
 2164 GOSUB 6000
 2165 FOR I=I8 TO I9:FOR J=J8 TO J9:K(I,J)=Q(1,1): NEXT J: NEXT I
 2166 GOTO 2161
2170      FOR J = 2 TO J1: FOR I = 2 TO I1
2180         W(I,J)=2*K(I-1,J)*K(I,J)/(K(I-1,J)+K(I,J))/(Z(I)-Z(I-1))
2190         S(I,J)=2*K(I,J-1)*K(I,J)/(K(I,J-1)+K(I,J))/(R(J)-R(J-1))
2200         IF P4>0 THEN S(I,J)=S(I,J)*(R(J)+R(J-1))/2
2210      NEXT I: NEXT J
2220      INPUT "DENSITY (kg/m^3) = ";R0
2230      INPUT "SPECIFIC HEAT (J/kgK) = ";C0
2240   REM    SET SOURCE IN Q ARRAY, DEFAULT IS 0
2250      PRINT "HEAT SOURCE (UNIFORM) =";
2260      INPUT Q(1,1)
2270      FOR J = 1 TO J1: FOR I = 1 TO I1
2280         Q(I,J) = Q(1,1)
2290      NEXT I: NEXT J
 2291 PRINT "ANY (FURTHER) NON-UNIFORMITIES? ";
 2292 INPUT A$
 2293 IF LEFT$(A$,1)<>"Y" THEN 2999
 2294 GOSUB 6000
 2295 FOR I=I8 TO I9:FOR J=J8 TO J9:Q(I,J)=Q(1,1): NEXT J: NEXT I
 2296 GOTO 2291
2999   RETURN

6000 REM SUBROUTINE FOR MODIFICATIONS OF ARRAYS
6030 PRINT "FROM I= ";
6040 INPUT I8
6045 IF I8<2 THEN I8=2
6050 PRINT "TO I= ";
6060 INPUT I9
6065 IF I9 > I1-1 THEN I9=I1-1
6070 PRINT "FROM J= ";
6080 INPUT J8
6085 IF J8<2 THEN J8=2
6090 PRINT "TO J= ";
6100 INPUT J9
6105 IF J9>J1-1 THEN J9=J1-1
6110 PRINT "ENTER VALUE TO BE USED";
6120 INPUT Q(1,1)
6999 RETURN
```

The subroutine at 6000 is used for input. There are checks to ensure that the values of the bounds set for the changes do not stray into the edges of the calculation zone. This is to avoid overwriting the effective thermal conductivities calculated in lines 2110–2150.

10.2 Applications with Standard-type Boundary Conditions

10.2.1 Rectangular intrusion

The first case we consider is illustrated by RUN 10.1 and figure 10.1. It is a solid with a rectangular lump cut out at one corner. The solid is subjected to fixed boundary temperatures and a uniform internal heat source. We can model this shape with the inputs shown in RUN 10.1, using the update described in section 10.1. It is also the solution of the problem of the steady fully-developed laminar flow in a pipe of square cross-section with a square intrusion in one corner.

There is one slight problem in interpreting the contour plots of this kind of shape. Because the values are known at the nodes and not at the boundaries of the cells, there is a 'smearing' of the contours around the intrusion. The contours are plotted as if the value of the temperature (or velocity) fell to zero between one node and the next, whereas we know that the drop actually occurs between a node and the edge of its cell. So you must imagine the contours next to the intrusion squeezed slightly away from the intrusion to get a more accurate picture. Modifying the contour-plotting routine is actually rather difficult.

There is one further point, about convergence. The variations in temperature no longer occupy the whole grid, so that our 'normalisation' in line 170 (multiplying by the number of internal nodes) may no longer be appropriate. It is worth monitoring the convergence closely to check that it is in fact complete.

10.2.2 Hollow square

RUN 10.2 shows the result of setting the viscosities to 1E10 (and the sources to zero, though this is not strictly necessary) in the region I = 6 to I = 12 and J = 1 to J = 7. This gives us the solution to the problem of a square-sectioned block with a square cut out of its centre, the faces being held at 0° Celsius and the interior subjected to a heat source. Alternatively, it can be seen as the solution of the fully-developed laminar flow in a duct with the cross-section of a square with a square hole in it. The contour plot for RUN 10.2 is shown in figure 10.2. Rather more detail of the corner – where it turns out that all the interesting things happen – is shown in figure 10.3 which uses an expanding grid in the x-direction and an inversely and contracting grid in the y-direction.

10.2.3 Non-uniform conductivity

We first try a very simple problem: that of the one-dimensional composite material. RUN 10.3a shows what happens if we set the conductivity equal to 2 from I = 2 to I = 6 and equal to 1 from I = 7 to I = 11. Not surprisingly, we get two straight lines (or nearly so!) with gradients inversely proportional to the conductivities. This is just Ohm's Law again, which tells us that the potential (voltage) drop across a conductor is proportional to the resistance.

That was easy. Now we consider a much more difficult problem. RUN 10.3b shows what happens if we have a square body heated from the outside, with non-uniform conductivity inside. Figure 10.4 shows the steady-state contour plot.

10.3 Non-standard Boundary Conditions

10.3.1 Specified-gradient boundary conditions

In RUN 10.4a we have made the gradient along the W face equal to 1 and the temperature on the E face equal to 0, with a uniform heat source. This is a one-dimensional problem and it corresponds exactly to what we did in section 4.5. We can use (with only the appropriate changes) the same modifications as we did there, and these are shown above RUN 10.4a. The line numbers are a bit different and we have to bend our rule not to modify the PLOT routine, as we have to overrule the interpolation for the boundary value at line 5300: this has already been done in line 4482.

RUN 10.4b and figure 10.5 show the result of using exactly the same modifications as for RUN 10.4a but now allowing the problem to become two-dimensional. If we check the values up the W face we can see that the gradients are indeed equal to 1.

10.3.2 Sine wave along an edge

If we look at RUN 10.5 we see the result of imposing a temperature

$$\sin(P3 * x/W1/2)$$

along the bottom (S) face of a square block. The modification needed for EDGE is shown (line 3660).

P3, you may recall, is π (3.14159..), set at line 1060 and never before used. There is an 'exact' solution for this problem

$$\text{temperature} = \text{sech}(H1/W1 * P3/2) * \cosh(P3 * y/W1/2) * \sin(P3 * x/W1/2)$$

To check the results of RUN 10.5 we have written a short program to generate the results of this formula: the program and the output are shown immediately after RUN 10.5 and figure 10.6 (the contour plot of RUN 10.5).

Incidentally, if you have not met 'hyperbolic' functions before, it will help you to know that cosh(x) is just shorthand for (exp(x) + exp($-x$))/2 and sech(x) is the reciprocal of cosh(x).

10.4 Modifications to the Contour Plot: Standardised Contours

If we want to modify the contour plot to give standardised contours, we need only specify the maximum and/or minimum value to be plotted. RUN 10.6 is for a solid initially at zero temperature everywhere and subjected to a fixed temperature of 100 on all its edges. Figure 10.7 shows the results at various times from 0.01 seconds to 0.63 seconds (a-f). In order to be able to compare the plots directly, as the minimum value is rising with time, we specify that all the contours should be plotted as if the minimum were zero, as it is at the outset. In this way the contours are always at intervals of 0.1 times the highest temperature, which will, of course, be the boundary value (here 100°).

This RUN happens also to be the solution of the problem of the flow some way down the wake of a 'bluff' body. Figure 10.8 shows a sketch of the streamlines behind the body, here a square, taken from the positions of the contours. Each contour plot is a cross-section of the flow, so the streamlines are drawn by joining corresponding contours, each cross-section being placed an appropriate distance (0.01, . . ., 0.63 metres) downstream of the square obstruction. The sketch in figure 10.8 should now be compared with figure 10.9, which is the picture of an actual flow behind a square plate. Not bad.

10.5 Epilogue

We have not covered anything but the simplest typical applications of the THC program. If you are interested in fluid flow, heat transfer or electromagnetism you will already have started messing about with the program to get more interesting results. That was the whole idea.

I hope you can see how little we have had to do to move from a very simple program – Program 7 – to an immensely versatile problem-solver. Even the gradient-type boundaries can be solved using the techniques of chapter 4. Anyway, good luck in the modelling of whatever problems it is you want to solve.

This is where you start to fly solo. Have fun.

Further Applications of the THC Program

```
PLANE GEOMETRY (0) OR AXISYMMETRIC (1) 0
NO.OF NODES IN X DIR'N = ?12
NO.OF NODES IN Y DIR'N = ?12
HEIGHT (IN METRES) = ?1
WIDTH (IN METRES) = ?1
GRID-EXPANSION FACTOR IN X DIR'N = ?1
GRID-EXPANSION FACTOR IN Y DIR'N = ?1
INITIAL (UNIFORM) TEMP (K OR C) = ?0
ANY (FURTHER) NON-UNIFORMITIES? ?N
SURFACE HEAT TRANSFER COEFFS.(J/m^2K)
NORTH BOUNDARY =?1E10
WEST BOUNDARY =?1E10
SOUTH BOUNDARY =?1E10
EAST BOUNDARY =?1E10
TEMP OF NORTH BOUNDARY (K OR C) = ?0
TEMP OF WEST BOUNDARY (K OR C) = ?0
TEMP OF SOUTH BOUNDARY (K OR C) = ?0
TEMP OF EAST BOUNDARY (K OR C)= ?0
THERMAL CONDUCTIVITY (W/mK) = 1
ANY (FURTHER) NON-UNIFORMITIES? ?Y
FROM I= ?1
TO I= ?4
FROM J= ?1
TO J= ?4
ENTER VALUE TO BE USED?1E10
ANY (FURTHER) NON-UNIFORMITIES? ?NO
DENSITY (kg/m^3) = 1
SPECIFIC HEAT (J/kgK) = 1
HEAT SOURCE (UNIFORM) =?0
ANY (FURTHER) NON-UNIFORMITIES? ?N
ENTER INITIAL TIME STEP ?100
ENTER FACTOR BY WHICH TIME-STEP IS TO BE ALTERED AT EACH STEP ?1
```

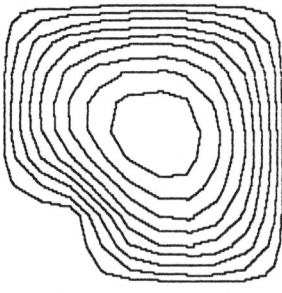

Figure 10.1

```
     TEMPERATURE   DISTRIBUTION AFTER 100 SECONDS


   X=   0    .05   .15   .25   .35   .45   .55   .65   .75   .85   .95   1

Y=1        **   1E-8  2E-8  2E-8  2E-8  3E-8  3E-8  3E-8  2E-8  2E-8  1E-8   **
Y=.95    1E-8   .505  1.01  1.31  1.49  1.57  1.58  1.51  1.34  1.04  .515  1E-8
Y=.85    2E-8   1.01  2.27  3.07  3.56  3.81  3.84  3.64  3.18  2.36  1.04  2E-8
Y=.75    2E-8   1.27  2.99  4.13  4.86  5.26  5.33  5.04  4.36  3.18  1.34  2E-8
Y=.65    2E-8   1.37  3.28  4.61  5.51  6.03  6.16  5.85  5.04  3.64  1.51  3E-8
Y=.55    2E-8   1.32  3.16  4.51  5.54  6.21  6.43  6.16  5.32  3.84  1.58  3E-8
Y=.45    2E-8   1.08  2.54  3.73  4.94  5.83  6.21  6.03  5.26  3.80  1.57  3E-8
Y=.35    1E-8   .548  1.20  1.92  3.68  4.94  5.54  5.51  4.86  3.55  1.49  2E-8
Y=.25    3E-8   4E-8  4E-8  4E-8  1.92  3.73  4.51  4.61  4.13  3.07  1.31  2E-8
Y=.15    3E-8   3E-8  4E-8  4E-8  1.20  2.54  3.16  3.28  2.99  2.27  1.01  2E-8
Y=.05    3E-8   3E-8  3E-8  3E-8  .547  1.08  1.32  1.37  1.27  1.01  .504  1E-8
Y=0        **   3E-8  3E-8  3E-8  1E-8  2E-8  2E-8  2E-8  2E-8  2E-8  1E-8   **

MAX=6.439412      MIN=1.00959303E-09
```

RUN 10.1

```
PLANE GEOMETRY (0) OR AXISYMMETRIC (1) 0
NO.OF NODES IN X DIR'N = ?12
NO.OF NODES IN Y DIR'N = ?12
HEIGHT (IN METRES) = ?1
WIDTH (IN METRES) = ?1
GRID-EXPANSION FACTOR IN X DIR'N = ?1
GRID-EXPANSION FACTOR IN Y DIR'N = ?1
INITIAL (UNIFORM) TEMP (K OR C) = ?0
ANY (FURTHER) NON-UNIFORMITIES? ?NO
SURFACE HEAT TRANSFER COEFFS. (J/m^2K)
NORTH BOUNDARY =?1E10
WEST BOUNDARY =?1E10
SOUTH BOUNDARY =?1E-10
EAST BOUNDARY =?1E-10
TEMP OF NORTH BOUNDARY (K OR C) = ?0
TEMP OF WEST BOUNDARY (K OR C) = ?0
THERMAL CONDUCTIVITY (W/mK) = 1
ANY (FURTHER) NON-UNIFORMITIES? ?YES
FROM I= ?6
TO I= ?12
FROM J= ?1
TO J= ?7
ENTER VALUE TO BE USED?1E10
ANY (FURTHER) NON-UNIFORMITIES? ?NO
DENSITY (kg/m^3) = 1
SPECIFIC HEAT (J/kgK) = 1
HEAT SOURCE (UNIFORM) =?100
ANY (FURTHER) NON-UNIFORMITIES? ?YES
FROM I= ?6
TO I= ?12
FROM J= ?1
TO J= ?7
ENTER VALUE TO BE USED?0
ANY (FURTHER) NON-UNIFORMITIES? ?NO
ENTER INITIAL TIME STEP ?1E6
ENTER FACTOR BY WHICH TIME-STEP IS TO BE ALTERED AT EACH STEP ?1


        TEMPERATURE   DISTRIBUTION AFTER 1000000 SECONDS


        X=   0    .05   .15   .25   .35   .45   .55   .65   .75   .85   .95    1
Y=1         **    0    1E-8  2E-8  2E-8  2E-8  2E-8  2E-8  2E-8  2E-8  2E-8   **
Y=.95        0   .447  .843  1.01  1.06  1.05  1.03  1.02  1.01  1.00  1.00  1.00
Y=.85       1E-8 .843  1.75  2.16  2.25  2.18  2.10  2.05  2.02  2.01  2.00  2.00
Y=.75       2E-8 1.01  2.16  2.63  2.60  2.31  2.14  2.06  2.03  2.01  2.00  2.00
Y=.65       2E-8 1.06  2.25  2.60  2.21  1.32  1.16  1.03  1.01  1.00  1.00  1.00
Y=.55       2E-8 1.05  2.18  2.31  1.32  2E-8  1E-8  1E-8  1E-8  1E-8  1E-8  1E-8
Y=.45       2E-8 1.03  2.10  2.14  1.10  1E-8  1E-8  1E-8  1E-8  1E-8  1E-8  1E-8
Y=.35       2E-8 1.02  2.05  2.06  1.03  1E-8  1E-8  1E-8  0     0     0     0
Y=.25       2E-8 1.01  2.02  2.03  1.01  1E-8  1E-8  0     0     0     0     0
Y=.15       2E-8 1.00  2.01  2.01  1.00  1E-8  1E-8  0     0     0     0     0
Y=.05       2E-8 1.00  2.00  2.00  1.00  1E-8  0     0     0     0     0     0
Y=0          **  1.00  2.00  2.00  1.00  1E-8  0     0     0     0     0     **

MAX=2.63424145   MIN=0
STEADY-STATE REQUESTED
PLOT YES
```

RUN 10.2

Further Applications of the THC Program

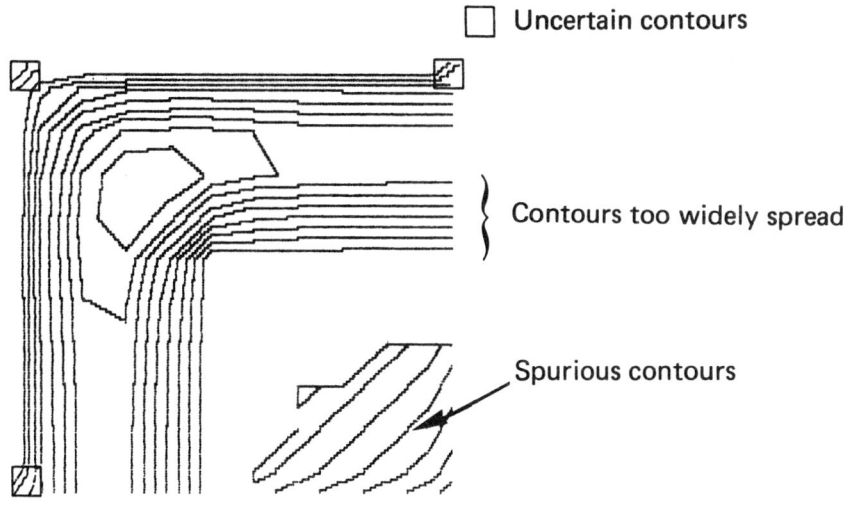

Figure 10.2 Results of RUN 10.2

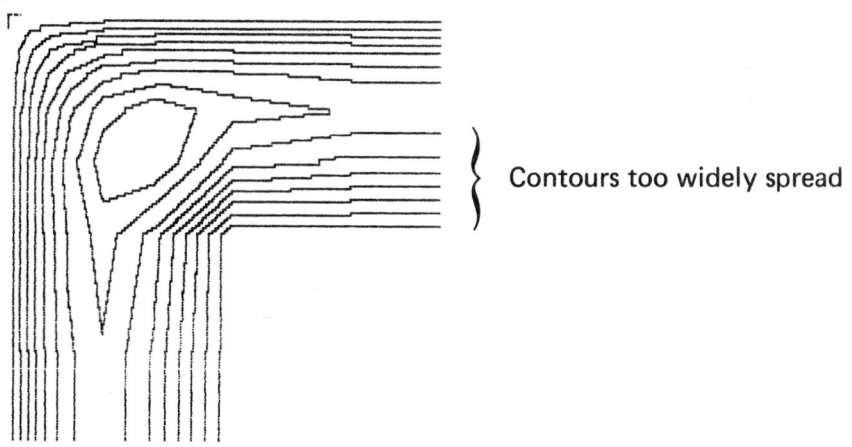

Figure 10.3 As RUN 10.2 but non-uniform grid

```
PLANE GEOMETRY (0) OR AXISYMMETRIC (1) 0
NO.OF NODES IN X DIR'N = ?12
NO.OF NODES IN Y DIR'N = ?3
HEIGHT (IN METRES) = ?1
WIDTH (IN METRES) = ?1
GRID-EXPANSION FACTOR IN X DIR'N = ?1
GRID-EXPANSION FACTOR IN Y DIR'N = ?1
INITIAL (UNIFORM) TEMP (K OR C) = ?0
ANY (FURTHER) NON-UNIFORMITIES? ?NO
SURFACE HEAT TRANSFER COEFFS.(J/m^2K)
NORTH BOUNDARY =?1E-10
WEST BOUNDARY =?1E10
SOUTH BOUNDARY =?1E-10
EAST BOUNDARY =?1E10
TEMP OF WEST BOUNDARY (K OR C) = ?0
TEMP OF EAST BOUNDARY (K OR C)= ?100
THERMAL CONDUCTIVITY (W/mK) = 1
ANY (FURTHER) NON-UNIFORMITIES? ?YES
FROM I= ?2
TO I= ?6
FROM J= ?2
TO J= ?2
ENTER VALUE TO BE USED?2
ANY (FURTHER) NON-UNIFORMITIES? ?NO
DENSITY (kg/m^3) = 1
SPECIFIC HEAT (J/kgK) = 1
HEAT SOURCE (UNIFORM) =?0
ANY (FURTHER) NON-UNIFORMITIES? ?NO
ENTER INITIAL TIME STEP ?1E6
ENTER FACTOR BY WHICH TIME-STEP IS TO BE ALTERED AT EACH STEP ?1




       TEMPERATURE   DISTRIBUTION AFTER 1000000 SECONDS

       X=   0    .05  .15  .25  .35  .45  .55  .65  .75  .85  .95  1

Y=1         **   3.33 9.99 16.6 23.3 29.9 39.9 53.3 66.6 79.9 93.3 **
Y=.5        1E-7 3.33 9.99 16.6 23.3 29.9 39.9 53.3 66.6 79.9 93.3 100
Y=0         **   3.33 9.99 16.6 23.3 29.9 39.9 53.3 66.6 79.9 93.3 **

MAX=100          MIN=1.33333317E-08
```

RUN 10.3a

Further Applications of the THC Program

```
PLANE GEOMETRY (0) OR AXISYMMETRIC (1) 0
NO.OF NODES IN X DIR'N = ?12
NO.OF NODES IN Y DIR'N = ?12
HEIGHT (IN METRES) = ?.2
WIDTH (IN METRES) = ?.2
GRID-EXPANSION FACTOR IN X DIR'N = ?1
GRID-EXPANSION FACTOR IN Y DIR'N = ?1
INITIAL (UNIFORM) TEMP (K OR C) = ?20
ANY (FURTHER) NON-UNIFORMITIES? ?N
SURFACE HEAT TRANSFER COEFFS.(J/m^2K)
NORTH BOUNDARY =?1E10
WEST BOUNDARY =?1E10
SOUTH BOUNDARY =?1E10
EAST BOUNDARY =?1E10
TEMP OF NORTH BOUNDARY (K OR C) = ?300
TEMP OF WEST BOUNDARY (K OR C) = ?300
TEMP OF SOUTH BOUNDARY (K OR C) = ?300
TEMP OF EAST BOUNDARY (K OR C)= ?300
THERMAL CONDUCTIVITY (W/mK) = 1
ANY (FURTHER) NON-UNIFORMITIES? ?YES
FROM I= ?3
TO I= ?6
FROM J= ?4
TO J= ?8
ENTER VALUE TO BE USED?10
ANY (FURTHER) NON-UNIFORMITIES? ?N
DENSITY (kg/m^3) = 1
SPECIFIC HEAT (J/kgK) = 1
HEAT SOURCE (UNIFORM) =?0
ANY (FURTHER) NON-UNIFORMITIES? ?NO
ENTER INITIAL TIME STEP ?.001
ENTER FACTOR BY WHICH TIME-STEP IS TO BE ALTERED AT EACH STEP ?10

    TEMPERATURE  DISTRIBUTION AFTER 1E-03 SECONDS


    X=   0     .01   .03   .05   .07  .090  .11   .13   .15   .17   .19   .2

Y=.2     **    300   300   299.  299.  299.  299.  299.  299.  300   300   **
Y=.19    300   262.  235.  225.  221.  220.  220.  221.  225.  236.  262.  300
Y=.17    300   234.  176.  153.  143.  139.  139.  142.  152.  178.  236.  300
Y=.15    299.  220.  145.  120.  109.  104.  101.  104.  118.  152.  225.  299.
Y=.13    299.  202.  127.  116.  108.  102.  90.5  88.3  103.  141.  221.  299.
Y=.11    299.  199.  126.  115.  108.  103.  87.6  82.8  97.4  137.  219.  299.
Y=.090   299.  199.  127.  116.  109.  104.  88.3  83.1  97.5  137.  219.  299.
Y=.07    299.  200.  129.  118.  111.  106.  92.8  89.2  103.  141.  221.  299.
Y=.05    299.  205.  132.  122.  114.  110.  104.  105.  118.  152.  225.  299.
Y=.03    299.  229.  164.  144.  137.  134.  138.  142.  153.  178.  236.  300
Y=.01    300   260.  232.  223.  219.  218.  219.  221.  225.  236.  262.  300
Y=0      **    300   299.  299.  299.  299.  299.  299.  299.  300   300   **

MAX=300           MIN=82.8542523
TIME OF NEXT DETAILED PRINTOUT ?.005
PLOT YES
```

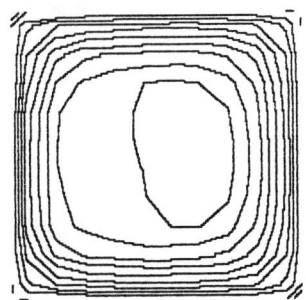

RUN 10.3b   Figure 10.4

```
4278 D(2) = D(2) + A(2)
4280 B(2) = B(2) + A(2) * (Z(2) - Z(1))


4482 N(1,J) = N(2,J) - (Z(2) - Z(1)) / 2

5300  REM
```

```
PLANE GEOMETRY (0) OR AXISYMMETRIC (1) 0
NO.OF NODES IN X DIR'N = ?12
NO.OF NODES IN Y DIR'N = ?3
HEIGHT (IN METRES) = ?1
WIDTH (IN METRES) = ?1
GRID-EXPANSION FACTOR IN X DIR'N = ?1
GRID-EXPANSION FACTOR IN Y DIR'N = ?1
INITIAL (UNIFORM) TEMP (K OR C) = ?0
ANY (FURTHER) NON-UNIFORMITIES? ?NO
SURFACE HEAT TRANSFER COEFFS.(J/m^2K)
NORTH BOUNDARY =?1E-10
WEST BOUNDARY =?1E10
SOUTH BOUNDARY =?1E-10
EAST BOUNDARY =?1E10
TEMP OF WEST BOUNDARY (K OR C) = ?0
TEMP OF EAST BOUNDARY (K OR C)= ?0
THERMAL CONDUCTIVITY (W/mK) = 1
ANY (FURTHER) NON-UNIFORMITIES? ?NO
DENSITY (kg/m^3) = 1
SPECIFIC HEAT (J/kgK) = 1
HEAT SOURCE (UNIFORM) =?10
ANY (FURTHER) NON-UNIFORMITIES? ?NO
ENTER INITIAL TIME STEP ?1000
ENTER FACTOR BY WHICH TIME-STEP IS TO BE ALTERED AT EACH STEP ?1


       TEMPERATURE   DISTRIBUTION AFTER 1000 SECONDS

       X=   0    .05  .15  .25  .35  .45  .55  .65  .75  .85  .95   1

Y=1        **  3.09 3.19 3.19 3.09 2.89 2.59 2.19 1.69 1.09 .399  **
Y=.5     3.04 3.09 3.19 3.19 3.09 2.89 2.59 2.19 1.69 1.09 .399   0
Y=0        **  3.09 3.19 3.19 3.09 2.89 2.59 2.19 1.69 1.09 .399  **
```

RUN 10.4a

Further Applications of the THC Program

```
PLANE GEOMETRY (0) OR AXISYMMETRIC (1) 0
NO.OF NODES IN X DIR'N = ?7
NO.OF NODES IN Y DIR'N = ?7
HEIGHT (IN METRES) = ?1
WIDTH (IN METRES) = ?1
GRID-EXPANSION FACTOR IN X DIR'N = ?1
GRID-EXPANSION FACTOR IN Y DIR'N = ?1
INITIAL (UNIFORM) TEMP (K OR C) = ?0
ANY (FURTHER) NON-UNIFORMITIES? ?N
SURFACE HEAT TRANSFER COEFFS.(J/m^2K)
NORTH BOUNDARY =?1E10
WEST BOUNDARY =?1E10
SOUTH BOUNDARY =?1E10
EAST BOUNDARY =?1E10
TEMP OF NORTH BOUNDARY (K OR C) = ?0
TEMP OF WEST BOUNDARY (K OR C) = ?0
TEMP OF SOUTH BOUNDARY (K OR C) = ?0
TEMP OF EAST BOUNDARY (K OR C)= ?0
THERMAL CONDUCTIVITY (W/mK) = 1
ANY (FURTHER) NON-UNIFORMITIES? ?NO
DENSITY (kg/m^3) = 1
SPECIFIC HEAT (J/kgK) = 1
HEAT SOURCE (UNIFORM) =?10
ANY (FURTHER) NON-UNIFORMITIES? ?NO
ENTER INITIAL TIME STEP ?1000
ENTER FACTOR BY WHICH TIME-STEP IS TO BE ALTERED AT EACH STEP ?1


      TEMPERATURE  DISTRIBUTION AFTER 1000 SECONDS

      X=   0    .1    .3    .5    .7    .9    1
Y=1        **   0     0     0     0     0     **
Y=.9      .106 .206 .328 .350 .304 .167  0
Y=.7      .397 .497 .686 .719 .605 .302  0
Y=.5      .498 .598 .801 .834 .696 .340  0
Y=.3      .397 .497 .686 .719 .605 .302  0
Y=.1      .106 .206 .328 .350 .304 .167  0
Y=0        **   0     0     0     0     0     **

MAX=.834103015  MIN=0
TIME OF NEXT DETAILED PRINTOUT ?2000
PLOT YES
```

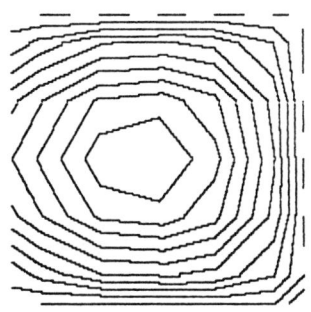

RUN 10.4b

Figure 10.5

```
3660  IF J = 1 THEN N(I,J) =  SIN (P3 * Z(I) / W1 / 2)
```

```
PLANE GEOMETRY (0) OR AXISYMMETRIC (1) 0
NO.OF NODES IN X DIR'N = ?12
NO.OF NODES IN Y DIR'N = ?12
HEIGHT (IN METRES) = ?1
WIDTH (IN METRES) = ?1
GRID-EXPANSION FACTOR IN X DIR'N = ?1
GRID-EXPANSION FACTOR IN Y DIR'N = ?1
INITIAL (UNIFORM) TEMP (K OR C) = ?0
SURFACE HEAT TRANSFER COEFFS.(J/m^2K)
NORTH BOUNDARY =?1E-10
WEST BOUNDARY =?1E10
SOUTH BOUNDARY =?1E10
EAST BOUNDARY =?1E-10
TEMP OF WEST BOUNDARY (K OR C) = ?0
TEMP OF SOUTH BOUNDARY (K OR C) = ?0
THERMAL CONDUCTIVITY (W/mK) = 1
DENSITY (kg/m^3) = 1
SPECIFIC HEAT (J/kgK) = 1
HEAT SOURCE (UNIFORM) =?0
ENTER INITIAL TIME STEP ?1000
ENTER FACTOR BY WHICH TIME-STEP IS TO BE ALTERED AT EACH STEP ?1


    TEMPERATURE  DISTRIBUTION AFTER 1000 SECONDS


    X=    0    .05  .15  .25  .35  .45  .55  .65  .75  .85  .95   1
Y=1      **   .031 .092 .151 .207 .257 .301 .338 .366 .385 .395  **
Y=.95     0   .031 .092 .151 .207 .257 .301 .338 .366 .385 .395 .395
Y=.85     0   .031 .094 .155 .212 .263 .309 .346 .375 .395 .405 .405
Y=.75     0   .033 .099 .163 .222 .276 .324 .363 .394 .415 .425 .425
Y=.65     0   .035 .106 .174 .238 .296 .347 .389 .422 .444 .456 .456
Y=.55     0   .039 .116 .190 .260 .324 .379 .425 .461 .485 .498 .498
Y=.45     0   .043 .129 .211 .289 .359 .421 .472 .511 .538 .552 .552
Y=.35     0   .048 .145 .238 .325 .404 .473 .530 .574 .605 .620 .620
Y=.25     0   .055 .164 .270 .368 .458 .536 .601 .652 .686 .703 .703
Y=.15     0   .063 .188 .308 .421 .524 .613 .688 .745 .784 .804 .804
Y=.05     0   .072 .216 .355 .484 .602 .705 .791 .857 .902 .925 .925
Y=0      **   .078 .233 .382 .522 .649 .760 .852 .923 .972 .996  **
```

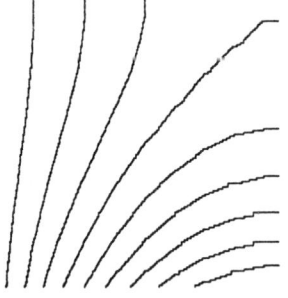

RUN 10.5

Figure 10.6

Further Applications of the THC Program

```
100  DEF  FN C(X) = ( EXP (X) + EXP ( - X)) / 2
200  P3 = 4 * ATN (1)
240  PRINT "     X =";
250  FOR X = .05 TO 1 STEP .1
260  PRINT  LEFT$ ( STR$ (X) + "      ",6);
270  NEXT X
280  PRINT
290  PRINT
300  FOR Y = .95 TO - .1 STEP - .1
320  IF Y < 0 THEN Y = 0
350  PRINT "Y=";LEFT$ ( STR$ (Y) + "      ",4);" ";
400  FOR X = .05 TO 1 STEP .1
500  A = 1 / FN C(P3 / 2) * FN C((1 - Y) / 2 * P3) * SIN (P3 * X / 2)
600  A$ = LEFT$ ( STR$ (A),4)
700  PRINT A$;
800  PRINT " ";
900  NEXT
1000 PRINT
1050 IF Y = 0 THEN 1200
1100 NEXT Y
1200 STOP

]RUN
     X =.05   .15    .25    .35    .45    .55    .65    .75    .85    .95

Y=.95   .031   .093   .152   .208   .259   .303   .340   .369   .388   .398
Y=.85   .032   .095   .156   .214   .266   .311   .349   .378   .398   .408
Y=.75   .033   .100   .164   .224   .279   .326   .366   .396   .417   .428
Y=.65   .036   .107   .176   .240   .298   .350   .392   .425   .447   .458
Y=.55   .039   .117   .192   .262   .326   .381   .428   .464   .488   .500
Y=.45   .043   .129   .213   .290   .361   .423   .474   .514   .541   .555
Y=.35   .049   .145   .239   .326   .405   .475   .532   .577   .607   .623
Y=.25   .055   .165   .271   .370   .460   .538   .604   .654   .689   .706
Y=.15   .063   .189   .309   .423   .525   .615   .690   .748   .787   .807
Y=.049  .073   .217   .356   .486   .604   .707   .793   .860   .905   .928
Y=0     .078   .233   .382   .522   .649   .760   .852   .923   .972   .996
```

'Exact' solution for RUN 10.5

```
5408 Z1 = 0

PLANE GEOMETRY (0) OR AXISYMMETRIC (1) 0
NO.OF NODES IN X DIR'N = ?12
NO.OF NODES IN Y DIR'N = ?12
HEIGHT (IN METRES) = ?1
WIDTH (IN METRES) = ?1
GRID-EXPANSION FACTOR IN X DIR'N = ?1.42857
GRID-EXPANSION FACTOR IN Y DIR'N = ?.7
INITIAL (UNIFORM) TEMP (K OR C) = ?0
SURFACE HEAT TRANSFER COEFFS.(J/m^2K)
NORTH BOUNDARY =?1E10
WEST BOUNDARY =?1E10
SOUTH BOUNDARY =?1E-10
EAST BOUNDARY =?1E-10
TEMP OF NORTH BOUNDARY (K OR C) =.?100
TEMP OF WEST BOUNDARY (K OR C) = ?100
THERMAL CONDUCTIVITY (W/mK) = 1
DENSITY (kg/m^3) = 1
SPECIFIC HEAT (J/kgK) = 1
HEAT SOURCE (UNIFORM) =?0
ENTER INITIAL TIME STEP ?.01
ENTER FACTOR BY WHICH TIME-STEP IS TO BE ALTERED AT EACH STEP ?2
```

TEMPERATURE   DISTRIBUTION AFTER .01 SECONDS

```
   X=    0    5.12  .019  .040  .070  .113  .174  .261  .386  .564  .818 .9999

Y=1       **   100   100   100   100   100   100   100   100   100   100  **
Y=.994 100    99.2  98.1  97.2  96.3  95.7  95.2  94.9  94.8  94.8  94.8 94.8
Y=.980 100    98.1  94.4  90.8  87.7  85.1  83.3  82.3  81.8  81.7  81.7 81.7
Y=.959 100    97.2  90.8  84.3  78.1  72.9  69.3  67.2  66.3  66.1  66.0 66.0
Y=.929 100    96.3  87.7  78.1  68.5  60.3  54.2  50.7  49.2  48.8  48.7 48.7
Y=.886 100    95.6  85.1  72.9  60.2  48.7  39.9  34.6  32.3  31.6  31.5 31.5
Y=.825 100    95.2  83.2  69.2  54.2  39.8  28.4  21.2  18.0  17.1  16.9 16.9
Y=.738 100    94.9  82.2  67.1  50.6  34.5  21.2  12.6  8.50  7.24  7.01 7.01
Y=.613 100    94.8  81.8  66.3  49.1  32.2  18.0  8.50  3.83  2.34  2.05 2.05
Y=.435 100    94.8  81.7  66.0  48.7  31.6  17.0  7.23  2.33  .724  .409 .409
Y=.181 100    94.7  81.6  66.0  48.6  31.4  16.9  7.00  2.05  .408  .083 .083
Y=0       **  94.7  81.6  66.0  48.6  31.4  16.9  7.00  2.05  .408  .083 **
```

TEMPERATURE   DISTRIBUTION AFTER .63 SECONDS

```
   X=    0    5.12  .019  .040  .070  .113  .174  .261  .386  .564  .818 .9999

Y=1       **   100   100   100   100   100   100   100   100   100   100  **
Y=.994 100    99.9  99.9  99.9  99.9  99.9  99.9  99.9  99.9  99.8  99.8 99.8
Y=.980 100    99.9  99.9  99.9  99.9  99.8  99.8  99.7  99.6  99.5  99.4 99.4
Y=.959 100    99.9  99.9  99.9  99.8  99.7  99.6  99.4  99.2  99.0  98.8 98.8
Y=.929 100    99.9  99.9  99.8  99.7  99.5  99.3  99.1  98.7  98.3  98.0 98.0
Y=.886 100    99.9  99.8  99.7  99.5  99.3  99.0  98.5  98.0  97.3  96.8 96.8
Y=.825 100    99.9  99.7  99.5  99.3  98.9  98.4  97.8  96.9  95.9  95.1 95.1
Y=.738 100    99.9  99.7  99.4  99.0  98.4  97.7  96.8  95.5  94.0  92.8 92.8
Y=.613 100    99.8  99.5  99.1  98.5  97.8  96.8  95.4  93.6  91.6  89.7 89.7
Y=.435 100    99.8  99.4  98.8  98.1  97.0  95.7  93.8  91.4  88.6  86.1 86.1
Y=.181 100    99.8  99.2  98.6  97.6  96.4  94.7  92.4  89.5  86.0  82.9 82.9
Y=0       **  99.8  99.2  98.6  97.6  96.4  94.7  92.4  89.5  86.0  82.9 **
```

RUN 10.6

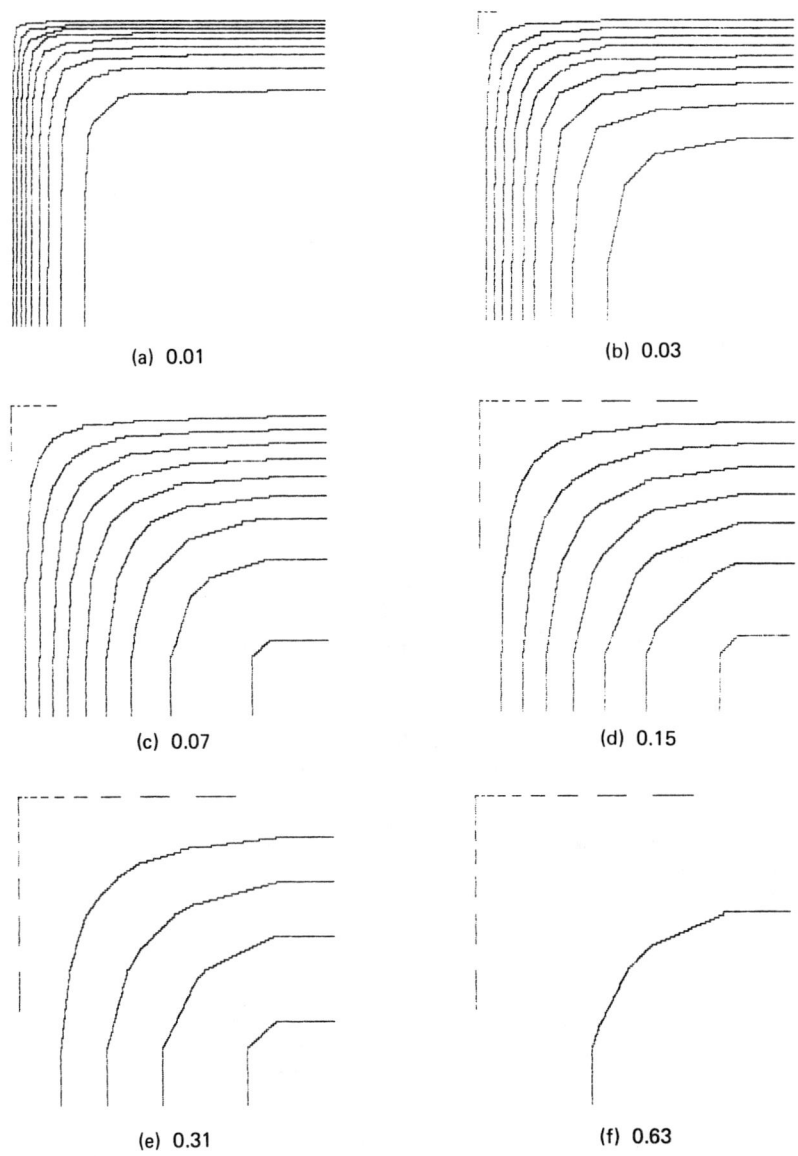

Figure 10.7

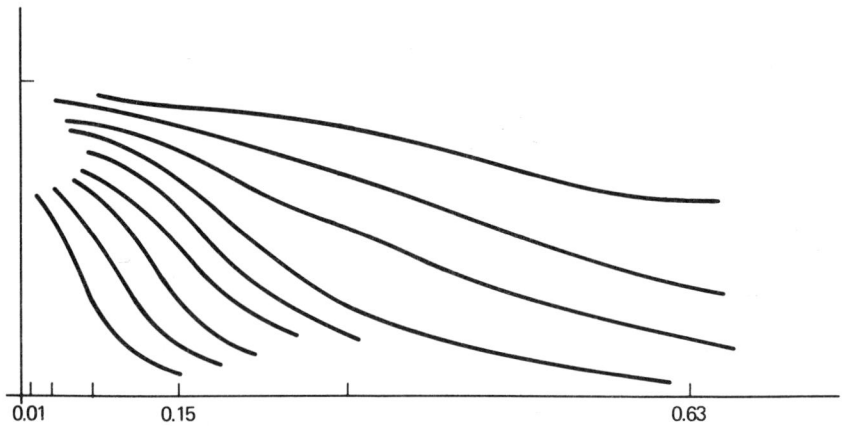

Figure 10.8

Figure 10.9

Appendix: Full Listing of the THC Program for the IBM PC
(Apple II modifications indicated in REM statements)

```
0    REM APPLE REQUIRES "LOMEM:24576"
1    PRINT CHR$(12) : REM CLEAR SCREEN - APPLE USES "HOME"
10   PRINT "IBM PC VERSION OF THE THC PROGRAM"
20   REM  DIMENSION ALL ARRAYS NEEDED
25       DIM A(12), B(12), C(12), D(12)
30       DIM K(12,12), N(12,12), O(12,12), P(12,12), Q(12,12)
35       DIM R(12), S(12,12), W(12,12), Z(12)
40   REM  MAIN PROGRAM CONTROL SEGMENT
50   REM  CALL START TO SET GEOMETRY AND GRID
60       GOSUB 1000
70   REM  CALL EDGE TO SET BOUNDARY CONDITIONS
80       GOSUB 3000
90   REM  CALL PHYS TO SET PHYSICAL PARAMETERS
100      GOSUB 2000
110  REM  SET INITIAL TIME- AND PRINT- INTERVALS
140      T1 = 0
150      PRINT "ENTER INITIAL TIME STEP ";
151      INPUT T2
152      PRINT "ENTER FACTOR BY WHICH TIME-STEP
              IS TO BE ALTERED AT EACH STEP ";
153      INPUT T8
160  REM  C2 IS CONVERGENCE CRITERION
170      C2 = .0002 * (I1 - 2) * (J1 - 2)
180  REM  SET ITERATION PRINT CHECK N7
190      N7 = 1
200      IF T2 > = L9 / 10000 THEN N7 = 30
210  REM  STOP TIME E1
220      E1 = 10000
230  REM  PRINT INITIAL DISTRIBUTION
240      GOSUB 5000
250  REM  MAKE TIME STEP
260         T1 = T1 + T2
270         REM  ITERATE TILL SOLUTION FOR TIME T1
280           GOSUB 4000
290         REM  UPDATE TEMPERATURES
300         FOR J = 1 TO J1: FOR I = 1 TO I1
320             O(I,J) = N(I,J)
330         NEXT I: NEXT J
350         REM  TEST WHETHER OUTPUT NEEDED
```

```
360        IF T1 > = P1 THEN GOSUB 5000
370        REM  TEST FOR STOP CONDITION
380        IF T1 > E1 THEN 430
390        REM INCREASE TIME STEP LENGTH
405        T2 = T2 * T8
410        GOTO 260
420  REM  TIME STEP ENDS HERE
430   IF T1< = P1 THEN GOSUB 5000
999   STOP

1000 REM    SUBROUTINE START  FOR GRID AND GEOMETRY
1010 REM    THERE ARE I1 NODES IN Z DIRN., J1 IN Y (OR R) DIRN
1020 REM    S9 IS A SMALL £, L9 A LARGE ONE
1030   S9 = 1E - 10
1040   L9 = 1E10
1050 REM    P3 IS PI, I.E. 3.14159...
1060   P3 = ATN (1) * 4
1070 REM P4=0: PLANE GEOMETRY/ P4=1:SYMMETRY ABOUT Y=0 AXIS
1080    INPUT "PLANE GEOMETRY (0) OR AXISYMMETRIC (1) ";P4
1090   A$(0) = "X"
1100   A$(1) = "Z"
1110   PRINT "NO.OF NODES IN ";A$(P4);" DIR'N = ";
1120   INPUT I1
1130   B$(0) = "Y"
1140   B$(1) = "R"
1150   PRINT "NO.OF NODES IN ";B$(P4);" DIR'N = ";
1160   INPUT J1
1170 REM    H1 IS THICKNESS AND W1 IS WIDTH IN METRES
1180   R1 = 0
1190    IF P4 = 0 THEN 1220
1200    PRINT "INTERNAL RADIUS (METRES) (0 FOR SOLID CYLINDER) = ";
1210    INPUT R1
1220   C$(0) = "HEIGHT"
1230   C$(1) = "RADIAL THICKNESS"
1240    PRINT C$(P4);" (IN METRES) = ";
1250    INPUT H1
1260   D$(0) = "WIDTH"
1270   D$(1) = "LENGTH OF CYLINDER"
1280    PRINT D$(P4);" (IN METRES) = ";
1290    INPUT W1
1300 REM F1, F2 EXPANSION FACTORS FOR GRID IN Z, Y (OR R) DIRNS
1310    PRINT "GRID-EXPANSION FACTOR IN ";A$(P4);" DIR'N = ";
1320    INPUT F1
1330    PRINT "GRID-EXPANSION FACTOR IN ";B$(P4);" DIR'N = ";
1340    INPUT F2
1350    IF F1><1 THEN D1=2*W1*(1-F1)/(1+F1-F1²(I1-2)-F1²(I1-1))
1360    IF F2><1 THEN D2=2*H1*(1-F2)/(1+F2-F2²(J1-2)-F2²(J1-1))
1370    IF  ABS (F1 - 1)< = S9 THEN D1 = W1 / (I1 - 2)
1380    IF  ABS (F2 - 1)< = S9 THEN D2 = H1 / (J1 - 2)
1390   Z(1) =  - D1 / 2
1400   R(1) =  - D2 / 2
1410    IF P4 > 0 THEN R(1) = R(1) + R1
1420    FOR I = 2 TO I1
1430      Z(I) = Z(I - 1) + D1
1440      D1 = F1 * D1
```

Appendix: Full Listing of the THC Program for the IBM PC

```
1450        NEXT I
1460        FOR J = 2 TO J1
1470          R(J) = R(J - 1) + D2
1480          D2 = D2 * F2
1490        NEXT J
1500   REM  INITIALISE O AND N ARRAYS
1510        PRINT "INITIAL (UNIFORM) TEMP (K OR C) = ";
1520        INPUT O(1,1)
1530        FOR J = 1 TO J1: FOR I = 1 TO I1
1540          O(I,J) = O(1,1)
1550          N(I,J) = O(1,1)
1560        NEXT I: NEXT J
1999        RETURN
2000   REM  SUBROUTINE PHYS FOR PHYSICAL PARAMETERS
2010   REM  R0 IS DENSITY, C0 IS SPECIFIC HEAT CAPACITY, SI UNITS
2020   REM  W ARRAY STORES CONDUCTIVITY TO WEST OF NODE (K W-P)
2030   REM  S ARRAY STORES CONDUCTIVITY TO SOUTH OF NODE (K S-P)
2040   REM  W AND S ARRAYS DIVIDED BY CORRESPONDING DELTA-Z
2050   REM   K ARRAY STORES THERMAL CONDUCTIVITIES
2060   REM  NOTE K ARRAY CAN BE SACRIFICED, USING TIME-STEP
2070   REM  K0 IS THERMAL CONDUCTIVITY (MAY NOT BE UNIFORM)
2080 INPUT "THERMAL CONDUCTIVITY (W/mK) = ";K0
2090 FOR J = 1 TO J1
2095      FOR I = 1 TO I1
2100        K(I,J) = K0
2110        K(I,J1) = A1 * (R(J1) - R(J1 - 1)) / 2
2120        K(I,1) = A3 * (R(2) - R(1)) / 2
2130      NEXT I
2140      K(1,J) = A2 * (Z(2) - Z(1)) / 2
2150      K(I1,J) = A4 * (Z(I1) - Z(I1 - 1)) / 2
2160 NEXT J
2170 FOR J = 2 TO J1: FOR I = 2 TO I1
2180    W(I,J)=2*K(I-1,J)*K(I,J)/(K(I-1,J)+K(I,J))/(Z(I)-Z(I-1))
2190    S(I,J)=2*K(I,J-1)*K(I,J)/(K(I,J-1)+K(I,J))/(R(J)-R(J-1))
2200      IF P4 > 0 THEN S(I,J) = S(I,J) *(R(J)+R(J-1))/2
2210 NEXT I: NEXT J
2220 INPUT "DENSITY (kg/m^3) = ";R0
2230 INPUT "SPECIFIC HEAT (J/kgK) = ";C0
2240   REM    SET SOURCE IN Q ARRAY, DEFAULT IS 0
2250 PRINT "HEAT SOURCE (UNIFORM) =";
2260 INPUT Q(1,1)
2270 FOR J = 1 TO J1: FOR I = 1 TO I1
2280    Q(I,J) = Q(1,1)
2290 NEXT I: NEXT J
2999   RETURN
3000   REM EDGE SUBROUTINE FOR BOUNDARY CONDITIONS
3020 PRINT "SURFACE HEAT TRANSFER COEFFS.(J/m^2K)"
3040 IF P4 = 1 THEN E$ = "EXTERNAL"
3050 IF P4 = 1 THEN F$ = "INTERNAL"
3060 IF P4 = 0 THEN E$ = "NORTH"
3070 IF P4 = 0 THEN F$ = "SOUTH"
3080 PRINT E$;" BOUNDARY =";
3100 INPUT A1
3120 PRINT "WEST BOUNDARY =";
```

```
3140 INPUT A2
3160 IF P4 = 0 OR R1 <> 0 THEN 3180
3165     A3 = S9
3170 GOTO 3220
3180 PRINT F$;" BOUNDARY =";
3200 INPUT A3
3220 PRINT "EAST BOUNDARY =";
3240 INPUT A4
3260 IF A1<1E-5 THEN 3340
3280 IF A1<1E6 THEN PRINT "FREE-STREAM TEMP (";E$;") IN K OR C = ";
3300 IF A1>=1E6 THEN PRINT "TEMP OF ";E$;" BOUNDARY (K OR C) = ";
3320 INPUT A6
3340 IF A2<1E-5 THEN 3420
3360 IF A2<1E6 THEN PRINT "FREE-STREAM TEMP (WEST) IN K OR C = ";
3380 IF A2>=1E6 THEN PRINT "TEMP OF WEST BOUNDARY (K OR C) = ";
3400 INPUT A7
3420 IF A3<1E-5 THEN 3500
3440 IF A3<1E6 THEN PRINT "FREE-STREAM TEMP (";F$;") IN K OR C = ";
3460 IF A3>=1E6 THEN PRINT "TEMP OF ";F$;" BOUNDARY (K OR C) = ";
3480 INPUT A8
3500 IF A4<1E-5 THEN 3580
3520 IF A4<1E6 THEN PRINT "FREE-STREAM TEMP (EAST) IN K OR C= ";
3540 IF A4>=1E6 THEN PRINT "TEMP OF EAST BOUNDARY (K OR C)= ";
3560 INPUT A9
3580 FOR J = 1 TO J1
3600     FOR I = 1 TO I1
3620         IF J = J1 THEN N(I,J) = A6
3640         IF I = 1 THEN N(I,J) = A7
3660         IF J = 1 THEN N(I,J) = A8
3680         IF I = I1 THEN N(I,J) = A9
3700     NEXT I
3720 NEXT J
3999 RETURN
4000 REM    SUBROUTINE WORK FOR CALCULATIONS
4010 REM    MODIFIED TO USE TDMA
4020 REM    C3 IS THE COUNTER USED FOR ITERATIONS
4030    C3 = 0
4040     IF T1>T2 THEN 4100
4050 REM N3 IS THE MAX PERMITTED £ OF ITERATIONS AT A GIVEN TIME
4060    N3 = 200
4070 REM    N(N4,N5) IS THE MONITORING AND CONVERGENCE CHECK POINT
4080    N4 = INT ((I1 + 1) / 2)
4090    N5 = INT ((J1 + 1) / 2)
4100    T3 = R0 * C0 / T2
4110    D3 = 0
4120     IF C3>N3 THEN 4560
4130 REM
4140 REM    HERE WE START TO SWEEP THE LINES
4150 REM
4160     FOR J = 2 TO J1 - 1
4170         R6 = 1
4180         IF P4>0 THEN R6 = R(J)
4190         R3 = (R(J + 1) - R(J - 1)) / 2 * R6
```

Appendix: Full Listing of the THC Program for the IBM PC

```
4200       REM    HERE WE USE THE TDMA ALONG A LINE
4210       FOR I = 2 TO I1 - 1
4220           Z3 = (Z(I + 1) - Z(I - 1)) / 2: REM    Z3 IS DZ
4230           A(I) = W(I,J) / Z3
4240           B(I)=-T3*O(I,J)-Q(I,J)-(S(I,J+1)*N(I,J+1)
                   +S(I,J)*N(I,J-1))/R3
4250           C(I) = W(I + 1,J) / Z3
4260           D(I) = - T3 - (W(I,J)+W(I+1,J))/Z3
                   -(S(I,J)+S(I,J+1))/R3
4270       NEXT I
4280       B(2) = B(2) - A(2) * N(1,J)
4290       B(I1 - 1) = B(I1 - 1) - C(I1 - 1) * N(I1,J)
4300       FOR I = 3 TO I1 - 1
4310           REM  MODIFY THE D(I) AND B(I)
4320           M1 = A(I) / D(I - 1)
4330           D(I) = D(I) - M1 * C(I - 1)
4340           B(I) = B(I) - M1 * B(I - 1)
4350       NEXT I
4360       N(I1 - 1,J) = B(I1 - 1) / D(I1 - 1)
4370       FOR I = I1 - 2 TO 2 STEP - 1
4380           O = N(I,J)
4390           N(I,J) = (B(I) - C(I) * N(I + 1,J)) / D(I)
4400           REM HERE WE ARE RECOVERING THE NEW TEMPERATURES
4410           REM     HAVING STORED EACH OLD TEMPERATURE IN O
4420           REM     D3 IS GLOBAL CHANGE IN N OVER THE ITERATION
4430           D3 = D3 + ABS(O-N(I,J))*2/(ABS(O)+ABS(N(I,J))+.001)
4440           IF C3>0 THEN 4480
4450           REM NOW DETERMINE MAX DN/DT AND MONITOR THIS UFN
4460           D4 =  ABS (N(I,J) - O(I,J))
4470           IF D4>D5 THEN N4 = I
4472           IF D4>D5 THEN N5 = J
4474           IF D4>D5 THEN D5 = D4
4480       NEXT I
4485     NEXT J
4490     C3 = C3 + 1
4500     REM    CHECK IF PRINTOUT REQUIRED AT THIS ITERATION
4510     IF C3 / N7>< INT (C3 / N7) THEN 4540
4520     PRINT C3;" SWEEPS AT ";T1;" S GIVE N(";
4525     PRINT N4;",";N5;")= ";N(N4,N5);
4530     PRINT "; CHANGE= ";D3
4540     IF D3>C2 THEN 4110
4550     RETURN
4560     PRINT N3;" ITERATIONS DID NOT ENSURE CONVERGENCE"
4570     PRINT "THE FOLLOWING RESULTS ARE UNCONVERGED"
4580     GOSUB 5000
4590     STOP
4999  REM   TERMINATE HERE IF UNCONVERGED.
5000 REM subroutine plot for output and plots
5005 PRINT
5010 PRINT
5015 IF T1>0 THEN 5140
5020 PRINT "The THC Transient Heat Conduction program"
5025 PRINT
5030 PRINT"Copyright 1986---Author and Programmer Dr Gordon Reece"
5035 PRINT"University of Bristol, Bristol 8, England"
```

```
5040 PRINT
5045 PRINT"Height =                    "; TAB(32);H1
5050 PRINT"Width =                     "; TAB(32);W1
5055 PRINT"Thermal Conductivity = "; TAB(32);K0
5060 PRINT"Density =                   "; TAB(32);R0
5065 PRINT"Specific Heat =         "; TAB(32);C0
5070 J$="no of nodes in"
5075 K$=" x "
5080 L$="direction = "
5085 IF P4=1 THEN K$=" z "
5090 M$=" y "
5095 IF P4=1 THEN M$=" r "
5100 PRINT J$+K$+L$;TAB(32);I1
5105 PRINT J$+M$+L$;TAB(32);J1
5110 REM insert a pause here if one is needed
5115 G$="plane"
5120 IF P4>0 THEN G$="axisymmetric"
5125 PRINT
5130 PRINT G$;" geometry"
5135 PRINT
5140 PRINT"     ";
5145 PRINT" temperature distribution ";
5150 PRINT"after ";T1;" seconds"
5155 PRINT
5160 PRINT
5165 C$="r="
5170 IF P4=0 THEN C$="y="
5175 I$="   z= "
5180 IF P4=0 THEN I$ = "   x= "
5185 PRINT I$+" ";
5190 A$=STR$(.5*(Z(1)+Z(2)))+"        "
5195  PRINT MID$(A$,1,4)+" ";
5200 FOR I=2 TO I1-1
5205 A$=STR$(Z(I))+"        "
5210 PRINT MID$(A$,1,4)+" ";
5215 NEXT I
5220 A$=STR$(.5*(Z(I1)+Z(I1-1)))+"        "
5225 PRINT MID$(A$,1,5)
5230 PRINT
5235 Z2=-L9
5240 Z1=L9
5245 FOR J-J1 TO 1 STEP -1
5250 IF (J-1)*(J-J1)<>0 THEN PRINT C$+MID$(STR$(R(J))+"        ",1,4);
5255 IF J<>1 THEN 5270
5260 A$=STR$(.5*(R(1)+R(2)))+"        "
5265 PRINT C$+MID$(A$,1,5);
5270 IF J<>J1 THEN 5285
5275 A$=STR$(.5*(R(J1)+R(J1-1)))+"        "
5280 PRINT C$+MID$(A$,1,5);
5285 FOR I=1 TO I1
5290 IF (I-1)*(I-I1)=0 AND (J-1)*(J-J1)=0 THEN PRINT" ** ";:GOTO 5360
5295 A5=N(I,J)
5300 IF I=1 THEN A5=N(1,J)+K(2,J)*(N(2,J)-N(1,J))/(K(1,J)+K(2,J))
5305 IF I=I1 THEN A5=N(I1,J)+K(I1-1,J)*(N(I1-1,J)-N(I,J))/(K(I1,J)+K(I1-1,J)
5310 IF J=1 THEN A5=N(I,1)+K(I,2)*(N(I,2)-N(I,1))/(K(I,1)+K(I,2))
```

```
5315 IF J=J1 THEN A5=N(1,J1)+K(I,J1-1)*(N(I,J1-1)-N(I,J))/(K(I,J1)+K(I,J1-1))
5320 IF A5<=1E-09 THEN A5=0
5325 IF A5<.01 THEN IF A5>1E-09 THEN A$=" "+MID$(STR$(A5),2,1)+"e"+STR$
     (INT(LOG(A5)/LOG(10)))
5330 IF A5<.01 THEN IF A5>1E-09 THEN 5345
5335 A$=" "+STR$(A5)+"          "
5340 IF A5>Z2 THEN Z2=A5
5345 IF A5<Z1 THEN Z1=A5
5350 P(I,J)=A5
5355 PRINT MID$(A$,1,5);
5360 NEXT I
5365 PRINT
5370 NEXT J
5375 P(1,1)=.5*(P(1,2)+P(2,1))
5380 P(I1,1)=.5*(P(I1-1,1)+P(I1,2))
5385 P(1,J1)=.5*(P(1,J1-1)+P(2,J1))
5390 P(I1,J1)=.5*(P(I1-1,J1)+P(I1,J1-1))
5395 PRINT
5400 PRINT"max = "+STR$(Z2)," min = "+STR$(Z1)
5405 A=FRE(A$):REM force " garbage collection"
5410 IF T2>1000*R0*C0/K0 THEN 5430
5415 PRINT"time of next full printout ";
5420 INPUT P1
5425 GOTO 5435
5430 PRINT"steady-state requested"
5435 REM contour plotting routine starts here
5440 IF T1=0 THEN RETURN
5445 L8=11
5450 PRINT "plot ";
5455 IF LEFT$(A$,1)<>"y" THEN RETURN
5460 GOSUB 9100
5465 X1=(Z(1)+Z(2))/2
5470 Y1=(R(1)+R(2))/2
5475 X2=(Z(I1)+Z(I1-1))/2
5480 Y2=(R(J1)+R(J1-1))/2
5485 FOR J=1 TO J1-1:FOR I=1 TO I1-1
5490 U(1)=P(I,J)
5495 U(2)=P(I,J+1)
5500 U(3)=P(I+1,J+1)
5505 U(4)=P(I+1,J)
5510 C(1)=Z(I)
5511 IF I=1 THEN C(1)=X1
5515 C(2)=Z(I)
5516 IF I=1 THEN C(2)=X1
5520 C(3)=Z(I+1)
5521 IF I=I1-1 THEN C(3)=X2
5525 C(4)=Z(I+1)
5526 IF I=I1-1 THEN C(4)=X2
5530 D(1)=R(J)
5531 IF J=1 THEN D(1)=Y1
5535 D(2)=R(J+1)
5536 IF J=J1-1 THEN D(2)=Y2
5540 D(3)=R(J+1)
5541 IF J=J1-1 THEN D(3)=Y2
5545 D(4)=R(J)
```

```
5546 IF J=1 THEN D(4)=Y1
5550 FOR K1=1 TO L8
5555 U1=(Z2-Z1)/(L8-1)*(K1-1)+Z1
5560 K4=1
5565 FOR K2=1 TO 4
5570 K3=K2+1
5575 IF K2=4 THEN K3=1
5580 IF U1>U(K2) THEN IF U1>U(K3) THEN 5635
5585 IF U1<U(K2) THEN IF U1<U(K3) THEN 5635
5590 L6=.5
5595 IF U(K2)-U(K3)<>0 THEN L6=(U1-U(K2))/(U(K3)-U(K2))
5600 X=C(K2)+(C(K3)-C(K2))*L6
5605 Y=D(K2)+(D(K3)-D(K2))*L6
5610 IF K4=1 THEN GOSUB 9400
5615 IF K4=2 THEN GOSUB 9500
5620 IF K4=3 THEN GOSUB 9400
5625 IF K4=4 THEN GOSUB 9500
5630 K4=K4+1
5635 NEXT K2:NEXT K1
5640 NEXT I:NEXT J
5645 INPUT P$:REM apple requires "GET P$:TEXT" instead
5999 RETURN
9000 REM subroutines for graphics at 9100 etc
9100 CLS:REM clear screen, apple hgr2 does this anyway
9110 SCREEN 2,,0,0: REM for apple use "HGR2"
9115 REM for apple use hcolor=3 to give white on black
9116 X8=640:Y8=200:REM X8,Y8 are screen dot-densities
9118 REM for apple x8=280, y8=192
9120 DEF FNX(X)=INT((X-X1)/(X2-X1)*(X8-1)+.5)
9130 DEF FNY(Y)=Y8-1-INT((Y-Y1)/(Y2-Y1)*(Y8-1)+.5)
9135 REM x1,y1 lowest values, x2,y2 highest values plotted
9199 RETURN
9200 REM draw an x-axis at y=d0 from x=d1 to x=d2
9205 X4=FNX(D1):Y4=FNY(D0):X5=FNX(D2)
9210 LINE (X4,Y4)-(X5,Y4):REM apple HPLOT X4,Y4 TO X5,Y4
9214 REM d7 notches
9216 S8=1
9218 IF Y4<5 THEN S8=-1
9220 FOR I=0 TO D7
9222 X6=X4+I/D7*(X5-X4)
9224 LINE (X6,Y4)-(X6,Y4-4*S8):REM apple uses hplot
9240 NEXT I
9249 RETURN
9300 REM draw a y-axis at x=d0 from y=d1 to y=d2
9305 Y4=FNY(D1):X4=FNX(D0):Y5=FNY(D2)
9310 LINE (X4,Y4)-(X4,Y5):REM apple uses HPLOT
9314 REM d7 notches
9316 S8=1
9320 FOR I=0 TO D7
9322 Y6=Y4+I/D7*(Y5-Y4)
9324 LINE(X4,Y6)-(X4+4*S8,Y6):REM apple uses HPLOT
9340 NEXT I
9349 RETURN
9400 REM move the cursor
9410 X7=X:Y7=Y
```

```
9449 RETURN
9500 REM draw a line to new (x,y)
9510 LINE(FNX(X7),FNY(Y7))-(FNX(X),FNY(Y)):REM apple uses HPLOT
9520 X7=X:Y7=Y
9599 RETURN
9800 REM join-the-dots routine
9805 REM array plotter for d6 points (x(i),y(i)), i=1 to d6-1
9810 FOR I=1 TO D6-1
9820 LINE(FNX(X(I)),FNY(Y(I)))-(FNX(X(I+1)),FNY(Y(I+1)))
9830 NEXT I
9840 X7=X(D6):Y7=Y(D6)
9899 RETURN
9999 RETURN
```

Note: If you intend to *compile* an Apple version, use

    9110 HGR

(that is, high-resolution graphics page 1, not page 2) and locate the machine code immediately above HGR1 — that is, at $4000. This is because the compiled code is longer than the interpretive BASIC and will not fit below HGR2.

All the programs will work on an ITT2020 using the Apple II listings. The pictures will be smaller: to correct this, set X8 = 360 in line 9116.

Index

adiabatic boundary 63, 64, 65, 77, 84
algorithm 25, 27
analytical solutions 1, 7
Apple II 4
Apple II compilation 121
axisymmetric problems 59, 86

BASIC 4, 5
Biot number 66
boundary 63
boundary conditions 42, 45, 64

cartesian coordinates 51, 59
cell 60, 100
cell Fourier number 56, 58
Computer Assisted Learning ix
contour plots 82, 87, 89
control volume 60, 62
convergence 15, 25, 59, 78, 100
convergence criterion 17
Couette flow 84
critical damping 49
cylindrical annulus 87
cylindrical coordinates 59, 87

density 51, 52, 75
dependent variable 10
diagonal dominance 32
differential equations 2
discontinuity 62, 64
divergence 27
dot product 52
duct flow 89, 100

electrical potential 3, 90
electromagnetism 53, 68, 102
elephant, classical 1
elephant, finite-difference 2
elephant, real 1
elimination 29, 34
energy conservation 51

equipotentials 90
Euler's method 11
exact solution 1
explicit method 55, 56

finite-difference equation 48, 80
finite-difference methods 7, 9 *et seq.*
finite-difference model 53, 62
fixed-temperature boundary 64, 66, 76, 84
flowchart 14
fluid flow 3, 53, 68, 89, 102
fluid mechanics 53
Fourier number 56, 70, 85
Fourier's Law 61, 66
free-stream temperature 76

gradient 8, 43, 67
graphics 21, 57
grid 10, 13, 62
grid expansion 74, 100
grid lines 60
grid spacing 74

heat analogy 63
heat balance 60, 61
heat conduction 3, 51, 61
heat equation 60
heat flow 62
heat flux 66, 101
heat source 51, 53, 75, 88
heat transfer 51, 68, 102
hollow square 100
hyperbolic functions 102

IBM PC 4
implicit method 55
independent variable 10
initial temperature 98
interactive program 19
interface 21
internal energy 61

Index

intrusion 100
isothermals 82
iteration 14, 16, 25, 29, 34, 43, 45, 57, 67, 78, 81, 88
ITT 2020 121

keyword 4

laminar flow 83, 89, 100
Laplace's equation 53
line iteration 80
linear interpolation 13, 62
linear systems 29
linearity 88

matrix 33
Maxwell's equations 3
mean-value theorem 8
membrane 53
mesh 47
monitoring location 78, 80
muckspreading 88

Navier–Stokes equation 53
necessary condition 25, 32
Newton's laws of motion 3
nodes 8, 100
non-uniform conductivity 75
non-uniform grid 47, 48
normalised residual 26, 80
numerical output 21
numerical techniques 2

Ohm's Law 63, 77, 98, 101
one-dimensional problems 51, 84
oscillation 27, 49
overdamping 49

parallel plates 85
partial derivatives 52
partial differential equations 3, 51
perfect conductor 64
perfect insulator 63
PET 5
phantom nodes 46, 77
point iteration 79, 81
Poiseuille flow 86
Poisson's equation 53
polar coordinates 59
portability 4
pressure gradient 53, 85
program 0 5
program 1 10
program 2 15
program 3 19
program 4 21
program 5 28
program 6 30
program 7 37, 82
program 8 42
program 9 44
program 10 46
program 11 57
program 12 58
program structure 5
pseudo-convergence 25, 32, 81

real line 7
residual 15, 16, 26
resistance 63, 101

sampling rate 49
scalar product 52
scientific notation 28
second derivative 14, 18
second-order problems 13, 18
SI units 52
simultaneous equations 33
sine wave 101
solution domain 42, 74
source term 53, 101
space derivative 51
specific heat 51, 53, 75
specified heat flux 66, 67
steady state 54, 65
streamlines 102
stresses 53
substitution 29, 34
sufficient condition 25, 32
surface heat-transfer coefficient 65, 66, 76
surface temperature 76

TDMA 36, 79
TDMA coefficient 78
TDMA improvement 40
temperature 74, 85
template 6, 28, 30
THC
THC program 68
THC program applications 82, 98
thermal diffusivity 54
thermal power 53
thermal resistance 63
Thomas algorithm 36
time 51

time step 70
tri-diagonal matrix 33–44
true convergence 25

unconverged solutions 81
underdamping 49
uniform conductivity 98
uniform grid 14, 18

unit vectors 52
units 52

variable coefficients 45
vector operator 51
velocities 84, 89, 100
voltage 64, 101

Wake flow 102

Software Diskette

A diskette containing all the programs included in this book for use on an IBM PC is available (ISBN 0-333-43937-6)

Details of prices and availability can be obtained from
   M. J. Stewart
   Publisher for Computing Books
   Macmillan Education
   Houndmills
   Basingstoke RG21 2XS